Praise for *Red-Hot Sales Negotiation*

"This book is spot on. From understanding pricing and pipelines, to providing guidance on personal demeanor, it takes a complex art, demystifies it, and provides simple yet powerful rules to negotiate by. It rings true with my own experiences."

> —Ambuj Goyal, General Manager, Information Management Software, IBM Software Group

"Goldner and McKeon have an easy, believable, and enjoyable way of writing that salesmen can relate to."

> —Lennard I. Carlson, Chairman and CEO, Modagrafics, Inc.

"This book explains the steps of a successful sales negotiation in simple language with relatable examples for each of the four steps. Goldner and McKeon recognize the real issues and focus on tips and techniques to make the outcome a win-win for both sides. After 23 years of selling software middleware and solutions, I specifically related to the price issue. The authors are able to explain how to deal with this issue by 'synthesizing' the deal so both sides win. I was trained by major corporations on negotiations skills, and this book contains several areas (for example, power questions and phrases) that were never mentioned or addressed before. I recommend this book as a 'must-read' for every salesperson who wants to build good client relationships while closing profitable business for his/her company."

> —Nadine M. Rosenbaum, IBM Program Manager

Red-Hot Sales
NEGOTIATION

EVERYTHING YOU NEED TO KNOW TO CLOSE DEALS, BUILD RELATIONSHIPS, AND CREATE WIN/WIN OUTCOMES

**PAUL S. GOLDNER
AND PETER MCKEON**

⁕AMACOM

American Management Association
New York • Atlanta • Brussels • Chicago • Mexico City • San Francisco
Shanghai • Tokyo • Toronto • Washington, D.C.

3 1257 01679 7853

Special discounts on bulk quantities of AMACOM books are available to corporations, professional associations, and other organizations. For details, contact Special Sales Department, AMACOM, a division of American Management Association, 1601 Broadway, New York, NY 10019.
Tel: 212-903-8316. Fax: 212-903-8083.
E-mail: specialsls@amanet.org
Website: www.amacombooks.org/go/specialsales
To view all AMACOM titles go to: www.amacombooks.org

This publication is designed to provide accurate and authoritative information in regard to the subject matter covered. It is sold with the understanding that the publisher is not engaged in rendering legal, accounting, or other professional service. If legal advice or other expert assistance is required, the services of a competent professional person should be sought.

Library of Congress Cataloging-in-Publication Data

Goldner, Paul S.
      Red-hot sales negotiation : everything you need to know to close deals, build relationships, and create win-win outcomes / Paul S. Goldner and Peter McKeon.
           p.   cm.
      Includes bibliographical references and index.
      ISBN-13: 978-0-8144-7354-2
      ISBN-10: 0-8144-7354-7
      1. Selling.   2. Negotiation in business.   3. Deals.   I. McKeon, Peter.   II. Title.

HF5438.25.G6417   2007
658.4'052—dc22

                                                                2006102134

Printing number

10   9   8   7   6   5   4   3   2   1

From Paul:

To the three women in my life; my two daughters Jaki and Elissa, who have always been there for me, and to the new woman in my life, Lynn Spiess, who is showing me the way forward.

From Peter:

To my wife Gaye: my best friend, my moral compass, and my inspiration.

Contents

Preface

Before you get started, we want to give you our perspective on what makes this book different.

First, this book is different because it is written by two great sales professionals, not one. My name is Paul Goldner, and I have been in sales since 1983, first in a computer training company that I founded, and now in a global sales training organization that I cofounded with my coauthor and partner, Peter McKeon.

I was able to grow my first company from zero in sales and $3,000 in working capital to one with $100 million in sales in just twelve short years. We were the second largest company of its type in the world.

During that period, I negotiated many a sale. There were times that I was very successful, and there were times that I was not. The good news for you is that I will share both my winning and learning (losing) experiences with you. You can learn from both.

My mistakes cost me plenty. You, on the other hand, can save yourself the agony of learning the hard way by simply reading on.

My partner and coauthor, Peter McKeon, is also a great sales professional. Peter has a great deal of experience to share as well. He is recognized throughout the Asia Pacific area as the most down-to-earth and talented sales trainer in the region, and he will draw on all that expertise throughout this book.

The second unique element of the book is that I am from the United States, and Peter is from Australia. We're providing you with a global perspective. What you will learn here will work in most corners of the world.

Most important, there are many books on negotiations, but this book is on sales negotiations only! And when you learn our perspective on sales negotiations, I think you will be pleasantly surprised. This book is written by professional salespeople for professional sales-people. It was not written for any other purpose.

You should also know that this book is based on our world-renowned seminar Red-Hot Sales Negotiations™. Red-Hot Sales Negotiations™ has been fine-tuned and perfected over the last ten years, and has been delivered to hundreds of corporations and thousands of individuals worldwide.

Acknowledgments

To Christina Parisi for all of her help and efforts.

To Mike Sivilli for his excellent management skills and pleasant management style.

To Debbie Posner for her excellent copy editing.

To Kerry Ashton for his great proofreading work.

Red-Hot Sales
NEGOTIATION

Part **One**

The Science of Negotiating

CHAPTER 1

What Is Sales Negotiation?

A sales negotiation is the bringing of a sale to its successful conclusion. It is not splitting the difference to close a deal, it is not having the client use their leverage to create a deal that is untenable for the seller, and it is not the seller using his or her leverage to create a deal that is not good for the client. It is not about getting lucky, or having a charming personality. There is a science to sales negotiation, and that's what we teach in this book.

When I first started negotiating, I thought of negotiating like a boxing match. My objective was to defeat the other person. Actually, my objective was to soundly defeat the other person.

I used to have a negotiating suit, I used to go out of my way to look a little intimidating, if possible, by not shaving, and I used to go through the same mental machinations that I imagine a boxer, a rugby player, or an American football player might.

What I soon learned was that my initial approach would do very little to promote my long-run, or even short-run, success.

A sales negotiation is much like solving a mystery. The client will give you clues as to the keys to success, and it will be your responsibility as a great salesperson to put all of the pieces together to solve the mystery.

As you will learn the more you negotiate (or as you may have already learned through your experience), negotiations rarely if ever work out perfectly. Let's take a look at why.

The Sales Negotiations Challenge

Let's say you are selling a copy machine, and that the list price of the copy machine is $1,000. Of course, you know that the customer is going to expect a discount, so let us assume that you are prepared to sell the copy machine for $900.

Before you leave the office to "close the sale," your manager pulls you aside and reminds you how competitive the market is, and tells you that under no circumstance can you lower your price to below $800. This is your absolute bottom line, and the point at which you will have to walk away from the opportunity.

So, you arrive at the client, review the merits of your solution, and the client agrees that you have a great solution for their business. The problem is that the client has a total budget for your copier of $500.

So, what do you do?

Your bottom line is $800, and your customer's maximum offer is $500.

This might sound like a difficult situation for you, and it is. But this is what the essence of sales negotiations is all about. I'm sure that you have heard that all sales negotiations or all negotiations must be win/win. If you are unfamiliar with what win/win is, it means that the negotiation must result in a win—a good conclusion—for the seller AND it must result in a win—a good conclusion—for the buyer.

While this is true (that all negotiations must result in a win/win), it is a somewhat naive, theoretical approach or statement.

The Value of the Relationship Exceeds the Value of the Sale

Before I tell you why win/win is a theoretical concept, I must acknowledge its theoretical accuracy. Selling, as you well know, is a relationship business. You do not negotiate in a vacuum. One of the unique elements of sales negotiations is that you must bring the current sale to a conclusion—but you must also continue to work with the client on an ongoing basis.

This is why every sales negotiation must be win/win. If you do not create a win for the customer, they have the option of going with another provider in the next sale. Or, if they elect to stay with your company, they may look to "get even" with you the second time around. A win for you and a loss for the customer does not create a sustainable, long-run relationship.

Likewise, a win for the customer and a loss for you (and your company) does not create a sustainable, long-run relationship. If your company is taking the loss, you will eventually arrive at one of two conclusions.

The first conclusion is that you cannot lose money on every sale and make it up in volume. An unprofitable deal is an unprofitable deal no matter how many of them you make. No company can continue to lose money forever, and soon you will realize that this is not a good relationship, and you will move on.

If you do not come to the realization that your relationship with the customer is unprofitable, you will eventually develop a large enough customer base so that you will be forced to choose between one of two customers: The first customer is the one that you have been working with over time and losing money on each and every sale; the second customer is a newer one where you have actually developed a profitable relationship.

As you reach both your personal and your corporate capacity, you will be forced to choose between a win/lose relationship and a win/win relationship. A no-brainer!

The next point is extremely obvious but important: There are times when the relationship is both a loss for you, the salesperson, and also a loss for the customer. Let's say that the customer has negotiated a very tough deal. In fact, the pricing in the deal is so low that you are losing money on each unit delivered to the client. In response to the fact that the deal is not good for you, you may elect to react in a very predictable manner.

You may start to think about how you can salvage the deal and make it profitable for you and your company. In order to do this, you start to remove certain elements of the solution that actually make the solution valuable to your customers. As you begin to remove more and more of the elements of your solution, the deal will migrate to a loss for the customer as well. They will not get what they thought they purchased.

You can try to remove smaller items in the hope that the customer will not notice. However, as you remove more and more from the original agreement, you may run the risk of a law suit as it becomes more and more obvious that you are violating the original terms and conditions of the agreement.

So now you are in a lose/lose situation. You are losing money on each transaction, and the products/services you are delivering to the customer are not meeting their expectations. In this case, you will both look to migrate to a new relationship, again having created a relationship that is not sustainable over the long run.

Creating a long-run, sustainable relationship should be the objective of every sales transaction, every sales negotiation, and every salesperson. And now we know enough to see that the only way to create a long-run, sustainable relationship is to create a relationship that is both a win for you and a win for the customer.

However, win/win, as I've already stated, is a very theoretical state. The reason is simple. If you go back to the example we were discussing, your bottom line was $800. The customer's top line is $500. There is no way either party can go any further. So what do you do?

The first reaction, by most novice negotiators, would be to split the difference. Let's close the deal at $650. However, as I have already explained, this is not an option. Your management will not let you go below $800 and the customer can simply not spend any more than $500.

You could, of course, walk away because of the fact that you appear to have a potentially irreconcilable difference. However, what does this accomplish? If you reflect on the sales cycle, you will see that this is a very wasteful option.

Most of us will have made a number of cold calls to first get an appointment with the customer. And we all know how much fun cold-call selling can be. Now that you have your appointment, you have to meet with the customer to understand his or her needs. You have to develop a proposal, present the proposal to the customer against a few of your top competitors, and finally win the sale.

Now you are here at the point of negotiation. We all know that all that work did not happen overnight. Rather, it was likely the result of a long, hard consultative sales process. Why would you want to waste all of that work and walk away from the deal now?

The answer is that you wouldn't. Or, at least, you shouldn't. This brings us to the primary reason that you purchased this book.

How to Synthesize a Deal

Sales negotiations are not about winning or losing. As we have learned, sales negotiations are about winning and winning. However, in order to create the coveted win/win state, you must become extremely adept at "synthesizing" the deal.

Returning to our example, we are at a deadlock. You cannot go below $800, and the customer cannot go above $500. Synthesizing a deal is the ability of the salesperson to figure out how to make up the difference of $300. Let me give you a simple way to do this.

When the customer tells you that their budget will only support a $500 purchase, they are likely talking about the current budget period. In this simple example, the salesperson should first take the time to understand the customer's budget limitation, then take the time to evaluate potential solutions to the $300 difference in price, and then propose a solution to the customer.

Virtually every deal will need to be synthesized in order to create a win/win outcome for the client and for you, and it is the seller's responsibility to synthesize the deal. It is never up to the customer to synthesize a deal.

Why? Because the customer can always revert to another suitable alternative (provided by some other company).

If you haven't already noticed this, the customer tends to commoditize whatever it is that you sell. By commoditization, we mean that the customer believes that your solution and competitive solutions are directly comparable alternatives. When the customer believes that your solution and competitive solutions are directly comparable alternatives, price tends to become the major factor in the sales process.

This also means that the customer will have very little loyalty to you or your solution. They will readily move to alternative solutions if you cannot meet their terms and conditions; especially the condition about price.

We, of course, know that there are great differences between our solutions and competitive solutions (or at least there should be if you are practicing consultative selling). The trick is to use the sales process to help the customer understand this.

My favorite example of commoditization comes from one of our clients that sell semiconductor manufacturing equipment. Semiconductor manufacturing equipment is fondly known as "tools" in the industry. Perhaps it is a mistake on the part of the manufacturers to minimize what they are selling by calling what they are selling "tools." You should know that these "tools" are extremely complex pieces of equipment that typically cost several million dollars per unit. And, these "tools" are bound together in an assembly line, called a "fab" in industry lingo, to make semiconductors, or what we call "chips." Fabs are even more complex because you have to get several tools to work together in an effective and efficient way.

We are trying to impress you with the complexity of the environment because we always marvel at the fact that customers in the industry, companies that we all know such as Intel and Samsung, tend to minimize the complexity of the environment, and tend to commoditize the equipment.

No matter what you are selling, the customer will try to commoditize it, making price the major defining factor in the sales process and the sales negotiation process.

The commoditizing of your product or service during the sales process and the resultant impact of price becoming the major defining factor in the sale is, in and of itself, a major negotiating tactic on the part of the customer. At this point, we simply want to highlight that the customer virtually always views what we sell as a commodity. This means that if we don't take it upon ourselves to synthesize the deal, the customer is not going to synthesize the deal for us. The customer views our product or service as a commodity, and will simply move on to the next best alternative outcome in the sales process.

Now we are in a position to finally complete our discussion of the sale of our copy machine. If you recall, our machine has a list price of $1,000. We wanted to sell it for $900 and we had a bottom line imposed on us by management of $800.

The customer's top line, on the other hand, was $500. They cannot go any higher and we cannot go any lower.

As we have already discussed, one option is to split the difference but that is not really an option since it will not work for either party. The second option is to walk away from the deal knowing that we cannot go any lower and the customer will likely find what they consider to be a good alternative. Neither of these options really works for us.

The third option is to synthesize the deal. This is a very complex discussion and we will devote an entire chapter to this later in the book. However, for now, it is important to understand that we, the seller, can develop a creative, win/win outcome by adding to or changing the negotiating variables to create a solution that works for both parties.

One simple way to do this would be to defer a portion of the payment to a second budget period so that they could pay the $500 now and the $300 at some later point. Again, we acknowledge that this is a simple solution but it does show you how you can synthesize a deal to create a win/win outcome from an apparently deadlocked negotiation.

At this point in the book, it is important for you to understand that every negotiation has within it a win/win outcome. The win/win outcome might not be obvious and it might not be easy to obtain but it is there. It is our job, as a professional sales negotiator to find that win/win outcome in every sales negotiation.

The Essence of Sales Negotiations

The goal of sales negotiations is not to win. This is where this book and this approach differ from all other books and all other approaches. We will teach you all of the strategies and tactics that are typically used in sales negotiations. It is necessary that you understand what your customer can do in the sales negotiations process, it is necessary for you to understand how to counter customer strategies and tactics, and it may also be necessary for you to use the same strategies and tactics on your side of the negotiation.

However, when you counter a customer strategy or tactic, you are doing it in the context of creating a win/win outcome. Likewise, when you use your own strategies and tactics, you are not doing it to create an unfair outcome for the customer. Rather, you are doing it to synthesize a deal and to position yourself to create a winning outcome for both parties.

The Role of a Professional Salesperson

Some time ago, I was on a plane on my way to deliver a seminar in San Francisco. I was reading a book written by Norman Vincent Peale. In case you are too young to be familiar with Norman Vincent Peale, he was an author, speaker, and minister. He wrote *The Power of Positive Thinking*, one of the best-selling books of all time.

The book I was reading was called *Stay Alive All of Your Life*. It was clearly not a book on sales, yet I learned one of the most valuable sales lessons I will ever learn.

In the book, Dr. Peale was telling a story of a man who had started a furniture store. Like many entrepreneurs, this man had to invest his life savings in order to start the business. Also like many entrepreneurs, the business was thinly capitalized, and got off to a rocky start. In a very short time, the business was on the verge of failure.

Our entrepreneur was also a member of Dr. Peale's church, and went to him for advice. He was very distressed over the state of his business, and he was looking for some insight that might turn the business around.

When talking to Dr. Peale, the entrepreneur told of a woman who came to his store every day. She was studying a piece of furniture that she probably wanted to put into her home. She would study the furniture from every angle, trying to imagine how it would look in her home. She was also probably trying to determine whether she could afford the piece.

The store owner became very frustrated observing his potential customer. He was, of course, anxious for the sale. The customer on the other hand, was very meticulous in her evaluation. What could the store owner do to hasten the sale? In fact, this was the question he posed to Dr. Peale.

Dr. Peale told the store owner that you cannot be successful in business or in sales if you think about yourself. Rather, Dr. Peale advised that the store owner must *first* think about his customer. The customer always comes first in sales. In order to think about the customer, Dr. Peale advised that the store owner get to know the customer, study the customer and her family and learn about their needs.

This is very sage advice because at the heart of professional sales and professional sales negotiations are needs—the needs of the customer. In sales, you cannot be successful if you do not understand your customers and their needs. Questioning skill, used to discover needs, is an incredibly powerful sales tool and an incredibly powerful sales negotiations tool. Remember this as we proceed throughout the book.

A sales negotiation is not intimidation. A sales negotiation is not some mystical process where you trick customers into an agreement that is good for you and not good for them. Sales negotiation is simply understanding the customer's needs, or what we call "interests," and then putting together or synthesizing a solution.

In our world, the world of professional sales, our negotiations can be very complex. However, every negotiation comes down to one simple point: Can you develop an understanding of the interests of the other side? If you can, you will have the information necessary to create or synthesize your deal. If you cannot, you will likely put yourself and your customer in a suboptimal position.

In order to create an optimal outcome, two criteria must be met:

1. The sales negotiation must be win/win.

2. The sales negotiation must serve the interests of both parties.

Optimal outcomes are not created by splitting the difference. Optimal outcomes are not created by developing win/lose or lose/win outcomes. Optimal outcomes are only created through hard work, by asking good, open-ended questions to understand the interests of your customer, and by using the information gathered to synthesize a deal.

Some Sage Advice

Creating an optimal outcome is actually not that hard if you are skilled. Let me tell you why. When I got started in professional sales, my mentor was actually my mother. Yes, she was the one who took me under her wing, and taught me how to sell. She was one of the best salespeople I ever came across.

One day, I asked my mother, as she was approaching retirement age, what was the one thing, over all other things that she learned over a very successful forty-year selling career. Here is her response:

"The customer will always show you the roadmap to success . . ."

While my mother was referring to listening skills when she made her comment, her advice also extends to sales negotiations. At the heart of every successful sales negotiation is the "interests" of the customer. We must work exceedingly hard to find out what these interests are, using high-quality, open-ended questions and listening to the customer's responses. Then we can use this information to synthesize a win/win outcome.

Returning to Dr. Peale and his advice, the first step in selling success and negotiating success is to understand the customer and his or her needs or interests. Once we have captured the customer's needs (in sales) or interests (in sales negotiations), an amazing transformation takes place. This transformation actually forms the foundation for your negotiating future.

The transformation we are referring to refers to your ability to create an optimal outcome for both you and your customer. The transformation we are referring to allows you to create the coveted win/win outcome that we positioned as only a theoretical state just a few pages earlier.

If you do not understand the customer's needs or interests, you immediately position yourself as a commodity seller in the eyes of the customer. As we all know, the major determining factor in a commodity sale is price. This is one of the major reasons that price is a major factor in sales and in sales negotiations. We don't take the time to do our homework! And if we do not understand the customer's needs or interests, then all too often, we, as professional sellers or negotiators, think that the customer has the upper hand.

The customer has the upper hand if, and only if, you do not take the time to understand his or her needs and interests. Once you have learned the nature and extent of the customer's needs or interests, you level the playing field; and this is crucial to your success in the sales negotiation process.

The customer has the money, which is what we need, and we have the solution, which is what he or she needs. If you handle the negotiation properly, it is not the one-sided event that we have all learned that it can be. And that is what we are going to show you how to do in this book.

Dr. Peale continued by telling our entrepreneur that all customers are like this one customer: *all* customers have needs. This thought alone levels the playing field in sales negotiations. It is critical to understand your customer's needs because only then can you find ways to help your customers be successful. And once your customer is successful, you will be successful as a result of the process.

Once again, this is true in sales, and it is true in sales negotiations. Earlier, we talked about the ability to synthesize a deal. From our perspective of readers and writers of this book, Dr. Peale is telling us that it must be us, using all of our skill, all of our thought leadership and all of our business acumen to make these deals not only work, but to structure the deal so that it will be both win/win, and build a lasting relationship between you and your customer.

With that thought, let's move on to the foundation of all negotiation—creating a win/win solution for both seller and buyer.

CHAPTER 2

The Principles of Win/Win Negotiation

Win/win is the only plausible outcome in a sales negotiation. Sales negotiations are different than other negotiations in that in most instances, the seller will want to maintain a relationship with the buyer after the current negotiation is over. We all know that when you are in sales you're in the business of relationships and that you must think about maintaining the relationship each time you sit down at the negotiating table. Unfortunately, many sellers use negotiating strategies that end up harming themselves in the long run or they suffer from misconceptions that prevent them from making win/win sales.

Potential Outcomes

Let's take a look at the four potential outcomes depicted in Figure 2-1, starting with a win for us and a loss for the customer (the upper right-hand quadrant of Figure 2-1) and explore the most common mistakes sellers make.

	FIGURE 2-1. WIN/WIN NEGOTIATIONS	

		BUYER	
S E L L E R	*OUTCOME*	*Win*	*Lose*
	Win	Both parties are satisfied.	Buyer will terminate.
	Lose	Seller will terminate.	Both will terminate.

Outcome #1: Seller Wins/Buyer Loses

Let's start out by assuming that a seller is contacted by a buyer who is looking to purchase a particular item that the seller has. The buyer is also under pressure to complete the purchase as their boss is concerned about a project that seems to be lagging. In this instance, the seller would sense that the buyer had a strong time constraint and she would use this leverage to close a very good deal for her company.

Let's assume that the buyer is requesting a discount of 30 percent but the discount has expired since they have not done business with the seller's company in quite some time. Since the discount has expired, maybe the buyer was asking for a discount of 30 percent but would have been happy with a discount in the 15 percent range.

However, our seller was not familiar with the principles of win/win negotiating and decided to really leverage the time pressure the buyer was under. The seller decided to close the deal at a 5 percent discount, giving a small discount but one that would not allow the buyer to feel good about the outcome of the negotiation.

What would happen when it came time to negotiate the next sale?

The buyer might not invite the seller and her company to participate in the next sale. They could simply end the relationship and start to work with another supplier. Because they decide to work with another supplier, the relationship with the current supplier would end, which is the point of our discussion.

Creating a win/lose outcome where we, as the sellers, win and the buyers lose, does not create a stable relationship. In all likelihood, the buyer will look to end the relationship on the very next transaction.

Outcome #2: Seller Loses/Buyer Wins

A second possible scenario is that the buyer would win and the seller would lose. This could happen using the same facts as in the prior case but removing the time constraints from the buyer and giving them to the seller. We could do this by assuming that the buyer could make the purchase either this quarter or next. However, the seller is at the end of the quarter and needs the sale to reach her quarterly sales goals. With the time constraint clearly on the side of the seller, the buyer could use the time constraint, along with their purchasing power and size to turn the negotiation against the seller.

Let's suppose that the corporation uses this power to negotiate a really strong price concession—a concession well in excess of the 30 percent requested in the previous example. In this case, the buyer negotiates such a strong deal that the deal is no longer profitable for the seller. What we have created at this point is a lose/win outcome. Here, there is a loss for us as the seller because the transaction was negotiated at a price less than the break-even price for the seller. On the other hand, the buyer has a big win because the corporation receives the product at such a price as to almost make it free!

In the short run, the seller and their company would have no choice but to live with the deal that they have negotiated. However, in the long run they could act to change the circumstance.

We are going to assume that the seller has become a student of one of our other books, *Red-Hot Cold Call Selling, Second Edition,* (AMACOM, 2006), and has a strong new business development focus. Under these circumstances, the seller would continue to add other, new clients to her sales portfolio and eventually reach the point where she didn't need to maintain a relationship with a company that does not believe in win/win sales negotiations.

Yes, we are actually advocating dropping buyers from your customer list if they do not believe in win/win outcomes.

When you are in business, you must make a profit. You may have heard the old story about the two guys selling watermelons at a watermelon stand. They are selling watermelons at a very low price to attract customers away from the competition. Their business philosophy is to lose money on each watermelon and to make it up in volume. In other words, they are hoping that increasing their sales will account for the fact that they lose money on each transaction. Trust us; this strategy simply does not work! Do the math!

You cannot lose money on each and every transaction and hope to turn a profit at the end of the year. Yes, it is true that very large companies can afford to sell products at a loss to gain market share and drive smaller competitors out of business or out of the market. But even large companies cannot do this forever. At some point, after the large company has gained the target market share and/or driven the smaller competitors out of the market, they will raise their prices to the point where they can turn a profit. In fact, they may actually be in a position to raise their prices to unfair levels—but that is a discussion for another book, a book not written by these authors.

In any event, the idea of selling watermelons at a loss and making it up in volume simply does not work. So, if the customer forces you to sell at a loss, you will reach the point where it is in your best interest not to do business with the account and find other, more profitable accounts to do business with.

Along these lines, we have spoken to and interacted with hundreds of thousands of sellers in our careers. It can probably be fairly stated that, in many if not most instances, the seller feels as though the buyer has more leverage in the negotiation.

While this statement simply is not true, and we will discuss why again and again in this book, it is certainly true that sellers *believe* it to be the case. (If you recall, we discussed in Chapter 1 why the playing field is, in fact, level. There, we suggested that it was the buyer's needs that actually level the sales negotiating playing field.) The reason we are bringing this up is because we want to give you a very effective negotiating tactic at this point.

Negotiating Tactic   Any time the buyer starts to push too hard in a sales negotiation, take out a blank piece of paper and draw Figure 2-1 for your customer. Figure 2-1 is our win/win negotiating table. In addition to drawing the table for your customer, take the time to explain to them that win/win is the only sustainable outcome.

Remember, the buyer needs us just as much as we need them. They have a need on their side otherwise they wouldn't be at the negotiating table. It is up to us as professional sales negotiators to make sure that we fully understand the customer's needs and develop a solution that best serves those needs.

It is in the buyer's interest to find the vendor that best serves those needs and then work with that vendor over and over again. The cost of switching vendors after each transaction is very high and this should give the seller additional negotiating power.

Please note that the cost of switching vendors is not a simple cost. It is a complex cost. Switching costs may include training costs for the new item, getting the customer/vendor procurement system to work smoothly, quality issues as the vendor learns more and more about the customer and the new relationship, and many other items. In a relatively large transaction, we have estimated vendor switching costs to exceed $50,000.

In any event, should the buyer negotiate a deal that is a loss for us, at some point, we will find it in our interest to move on and find other, more profitable customers to work with.

So, at this point, we have seen in Outcome #1 that a win for us and a loss for the customer will simply not work. The customer will move on to other vendors. Also, a win for the customer and a loss for us, Outcome #2, places the relationship in exactly the same position. At some point, we will realize that there are better customers for us in the market and we will simply move on. And this brings us to our third outcome: lose/lose.

Outcome #3: Seller Loses/Buyer Loses

Here, let us assume that the customer has negotiated a very hard deal for us. They have created a win for them and a loss for us. Now, we are in a losing transaction. However, we must still complete the transaction.

One possible outcome to this situation is that we could respond to this situation, selling at a loss, by trying to remove services from the transaction so as to make it potentially, minimally profitable for us. We could ship to the customer after all other orders have been shipped. We could put our least experienced consultants on the project. We could not deliver the training we had agreed to, and we could take other actions in an attempt to make the transaction work for us.

In our attempt to make the transaction work for us, we could turn the win for the customer into a loss for the customer because we will not be delivering according to their expectations. As such, we took the win (for the customer) and loss (for us) transaction and moved it to the lose/lose quadrant. Now, we have a loss for us and a loss for the customer.

In this case, we will look to move to other, more profitable relationships and the customer will look to move on to more reliable suppliers. So, lose/lose is really no different that either win/lose or lose/win. All three relationships are unstable. In fact, saying that a relationship is unstable is actually an oxymoron. The word "relationship" implies an ongoing and recurring state and the word "unstable" implies just the opposite. In any event, all three outcomes, win/lose, lose/win and lose/lose create a situation that will not promote a lasting state where you get to work with the customer over and over again. On the customer side, it will not create a lasting relationship either and the customer will have to move to another provider and incur the cost of switching vendors, which can often be significant.

At this point, we have only one outcome left and that is win/win. Because the other three outcomes do not create a lasting relationship between us and the customer, it is in our best interest to always create win/win outcomes.

Likewise, it is in the customer's interest as well. First, if they are happy with the work that you do for them, why would they want to switch to another, potentially less reliable supplier? Also, why would they want to incur the cost of switching from one vendor to the next? As noted above, this cost can often be significant. The answer to the question is, of course, that they would not want to switch. The customer also benefits from a win/win outcome.

So, it is in our interest to create a win/win outcome and it is in the customer's interest as well.

Outcome #4: Seller Wins/Buyer Wins

As we've said before, many salespeople believe that the buyer has all the leverage in a sales negotiation. This is simply not true. While the buyer *could* switch from vendor to vendor in search of the best price, this constant switching becomes costly, and productivity often suffers as well. Also, as the seller you know that quality of the products or services is not the same from vendor to vendor. You know, from planning your sale, that your product offers unique value to the customer. This unique value is your leverage.

Also, in sales, it is not uncommon for the customer to negotiate with you *after* they have made their vendor selection. Once this is the case, we clearly hold the upper hand. However whether the customer has selected you (definitively) or not, you still hold the key to the successful application of your product or service to the customer's business. It is our contention that the value of the solution is the great equalizer in sales negotiations.

We shouldn't have to write this next section but in reality, we know that we do. Win/win actually means a win for the customer but it also means *a win for your company*. You may be wondering why eroding your sales margin is a loss for you. It is clearly a loss for the company but why is it a loss for the individual salesperson, especially if your commission plan is centered on gross sales and not gross profit.

The reason is that sales is a team sport. Mr. Spock, of Star Trek fame, said it first: "the needs of the many outweigh the needs of the few."

In sales, the most important objectives are corporate objectives—

achieving the corporate sales goal and the corporate margin goal. If the company does not achieve its objectives, it is unlikely that you will achieve yours. In the extreme case, the company will go out of business and be unable to pay your salary and/or commissions.

The Salesperson Must Create the Win/Win

All too often, we see sales professionals interpret the word "win" as "closing the sale." While closing the sale is good, it is actually not the complete objective in a sales negotiation from our perspective. The complete objective from our perspective is to close the sale and to close the sale in a manner that is rewarding to our business. And, this brings us to another significant point.

Many salespeople don't realize that it is their job to create the win/win. Win/win outcomes don't happen on their own. Sales negotiations are often so difficult because creating a win/win outcome is really not that easy! In fact, creating a win/win outcome requires a lot of skill on the part of the seller. The reason I am focused on the seller is because it is our responsibility to create the win/win outcome. We cannot rely on the customer to do this for us. If we can't create a win/win outcome, the customer will likely move on to another supplier who can.

So, how do we create a win/win outcome? This is the subject of the next segment of this chapter.

How to Create a Win/Win Outcome

Step #1: Get the Customer to Buy into the Idea of Win/Win

The first step in creating a win/win outcome is to get the customer to buy into the concept of win/win negotiations. The way we do this is to simply draw the win/win diagram (Figure 2-1) for the customer and discuss the potential outcomes with them. If you walk them through the discussion we outlined above, that should be enough to move them

over to your side. If you can't get them to support the idea of a win/
win outcome, the customer will usually create a win for them and a
loss for us. As you saw in our previous discussion, this creates an
unstable environment and over time, we will be able to find other
customers to replace the one that will not support a win/win outcome.

Step #2: Identify the Objectives of the Customer in the Sales Negotiation

So, let's say that the customer does support the concept of win/win.
The question then becomes how do we actually make this happen?
There are a number of things that we can do at this point. The first of
those things is to "meet the objectives of the other side."

It is important that we take a moment to study the meaning of the
word "objectives" in the prior paragraph.

When you are in the sales discovery phase of the sales process,
your goal is to use quality, open-ended questions to determine the
customer's needs; what they are trying to accomplish by buying a product or service like yours.

By way of example, let's suppose you are selling a computer to a
small business owner. Let's assume that the small business owner
uses a manual system to keep track of their accounting records.
Clearly, this would be an ineffective way of doing things.

As the computer sales person, you would use good, open-ended
questions to learn that the small business owner is using a manual
system to manage their accounting system. If you kept asking questions, good open-ended questions, you might also learn that the prospect's biggest challenge in growing their business and growing their
revenue base is a lack of time. The owner is so busy doing the accounting for the business that they have no time to go out and solicit new
customers. At a minimum, they might have insufficient time to solicit
new customers.

Upon learning this, and other things by asking your questions,
you might come up with an idea that the customer should purchase a

computer from you, and load it with some good accounting software to automate that portion of their business. The end result of the purchase would be to give the owner more time to develop new business.

Using this example, we could say that the needs of the customer in this case were to purchase a computer, and to automate the accounting function with the goal of reducing the owner's investment of time in the accounting area and increase the time available for sales.

Now, we get to the negotiating table. What the prospect might do in a case like this is locate other potential computer vendors to buy from so that he can get the lowest price for the computer. In the sales negotiation, this would be considered the "position" of the negotiator or the buyer.

The "position" is defined as "what is the buyer asking for in the sales negotiation?" In this case, they are asking for a good price so you could say that the position of the buyer is to get a good price on the computer.

However, the position is what the buyer is really asking for. They usually tell you this loud and clear at the start of the negotiation. What you need to do at this point is to help the buyer understand what they are really looking for as an outcome of the negotiation process.

In this particular case, the buyer is looking to implement a computerized accounting system so that they can reduce their time investment in accounting work and increase their time investment in sales work. This latter point is often unstated on the part of the buyer and is known as their "interests".

"Interests" are what the buyer is really looking for as an outcome of the negotiation process. If you consider that the proper implementation of the accounting system would allow the owner to sell much, much more than they could otherwise, and compare that to any potential discount any seller in the market could offer, you should be able to imagine that the buyer would be much better off with the successful implementation of the solution than they would with any price concession they could achieve. In all honesty, even if they could get the computer for free, the cost savings here would pale in comparison to the benefit of increased sales in connection with the proper implementation of the solution.

It is the good, open-ended questions in the sales negotiation process that allow you and the buyer to re-discover the buyer's true needs (interests) in the sales negotiations process.

Also remember that you must be tactful in how you lead the buyer to the conclusion that their interests are more important than their positions. The natural reaction to the purchase of a product or service is to get it for the lowest price. The best outcome is to develop an optimal solution and achieve one's business objectives. Questions are the tools that you would use at this stage of the negotiation process to guide and lead the buyer to the correct conclusion; the conclusion that is in their best long run interest.

In our sales seminars, we often say that there are three major events in the sales process. The first major event is when you pick up the phone to make an appointment with your prospect. This is otherwise known as prospecting for new business.

The second major event is when you are sitting face-to-face with the customer in a discovery meeting. Discovery meetings are meetings used to "discover" the needs of the customer or prospect.

The final major event in sales is when you sit down with the customer to negotiate the close of a sale.

In our seminars, we often liken these events to Olympic events. Imagine that you are going to compete in the next Olympic Games. Would you prepare for your event? Of course you would!

You would prepare and prepare. In fact, I would assume that your preparation would begin at the start of the close of the prior Olympic Games. In other words, you would likely prepare for your event for almost a four-year period.

In sales, we have three Olympic events: picking up the phone to make an appointment with your prospects, the discovery meetings where you work with the customer to understand their needs, and the negotiating meeting where you also work with the customer but this time to understand their interests in the sales negotiation.

To prepare for a prospecting call, we suggest that you have a well-developed prospecting script. This topic is discussed in depth in Paul's earlier book, *Red-Hot Cold Call Selling*, in Chapter 7, "Anatomy of a Cold Call." To prepare for a face-to-face discovery meeting, we suggest that you have a list of five or six good, open-ended discovery questions that you can use to learn the needs of the customer in the sales process.

Finally, to prepare for your sales negotiation, you ought to do the same as in the sales discovery process. Part of your preparation in the sales negotiation process ought to be to develop a list of negotiation discovery questions so that you can learn the interests of the customer in the sales negotiation process. Your list of negotiation discovery questions is going to be the focus of Chapter 8 of this book.

Learning the interests of the customer in the negotiation process will go a long way to helping you create a win/win outcome.

Some Final Thoughts on Interests and Positions

Acting on the basis of positions will often produce suboptimal or undesired outcomes in the sales negotiation process. In fact, acting on positions may not even lead to a successful conclusion of the negotiation at all.

Often we are asked in our seminars, "Why doesn't the customer take the time to really understand what both parties are trying to achieve with this transaction?"

The answer to this question is quite simple. It is not their job to learn about the interests in a sales negotiation. This is *our* job. Remember, if we do not do a good job of understanding the interests of the customer, we could create a suboptimal outcome to the negotiation. Or, the customer could simply move on to another provider.

So, it should be pretty clear at this point that it is our job to understand the differences between interests and positions and it is also our job to make sure we determine the interests of the customer as early in the sales negotiations process as possible. And we do this, of course, by asking power negotiation questions.

This chapter was all about creating a win/win outcome. Hopefully, we have shown you that the idea of a win/win outcome is not some pie-in-the-sky concept, but rather, a very concrete concept that we can apply to our sales negotiations strategy. Win/win is also crucial for our ongoing success in the sales profession.

CHAPTER 3

Creating a Solution That Benefits Your Company

What does it mean to benefit your company? We already know that it doesn't mean simply closing the sale. It actually means more than that. It doesn't even mean getting the highest possible price for your product or services. Many other issues are involved in creating a benefit.

There are a number of factors that enter into any sales negotiation. Nine of these factors are listed below:

1. Price

2. Payment terms

3. Contract volume

4. Contract duration

5. Delivery schedule

6. Product or service options

7. Post-sale service and support

8. Training

9. Other resources that you can bring to bear for the customer

While this is clearly a generic list, and there could be other items to negotiate that are specific to your business, it does raise two interesting points.

First, when we talk about a win for our company, we can see that it means that the sales price in the contract results in a profit for our company. And we are not talking about a gross margin profit (sales minus cost of sales), we are talking about a fully loaded profit (sales minus cost of sales minus the selling, general, and administrative costs allocated to the sale of one unit of your product or service). As you can see, there is a big difference between gross margin profit and fully loaded profit.

So, a win for us means that we not only close the sale but we also close the sale at a price which results in a fully loaded profit. And, what about payment terms? Payment terms are an important part of the transaction as well. In fact, there are a number of key elements to any sales negotiation and we suggest that a win for the selling company means that the combination of negotiation variables, the nine points listed above, result in a win for your company.

To develop a win for your company actually requires a great deal of thought and planning on your part. What we think you need to do is understand what a "win" means for your company in terms of each of the nine variables listed above. We have already acknowledged that there may be other variables in your business, so if your list contains eleven items or seven items instead of the nine that we suggest that's fine too. Whatever is on your list of negotiation variables, you need to understand each of the items on the list and you also need to understand what constitutes a win and what would be a loss to your company for each item on the list.

In order to do this, you must have a list, which brings us to another major negotiating point.

Negotiating Tactic   The first step in preparing for a sales negotiation is to make a list of the variables affecting the negotiation.

We have provided a generic list above and this list should be customized for use in your business. As we have already noted, you need to understand what constitutes a good outcome and what constitutes a poor outcome for each item in the list.

To be a good salesperson, you must successfully assert your company's needs. When we say that you must "assert your company's needs," what we are suggesting is that the combination of outcomes for your negotiation variables ought to be a net positive result for your company. This means not only negotiating a price that results in a fully loaded profit for your company, but also making certain that the outcomes for the other negotiating variables do not take the winning outcome you created for price and make the overall transaction a loss.

For example, suppose that you negotiate a good price but the customer insists on payment terms of 180 days. This is six months, or one half a year. And let's suppose that payment terms in your industry are normally 30 days. In this case, the five-month extended payment terms may take this transaction from a win to a loss and may not be a good transaction for your company. So, "asserting your company's needs" requires that you know your company's needs in the first place.

A win/win does not mean that the outcome of every variable needs to fall within the positive range. There can be both positive and negative outcomes in the list of negotiation variables as long as the net result of the positive and negative factors results in a win for your company.

For example, when you sell one of your products, it can normally be delivered with anywhere from one to five days of training, at the discretion of the salesperson. Let's suppose that the customer requires ten days of training and does not want to pay extra for the five days outside of your discretionary range. If you agree to the ten days, that is fine as long as the other negotiating variables are positive enough to support the negative outcome in the training area (the additional cost to your company for the extra five days).

Negotiating Tactic It is actually not sufficient to just make a list of the negotiating variables for your business. In addition to making the list, you need to rank each of the variables in order of importance to your company (in our generic list, from one to nine). And, once you have ranked the variables, you should then understand what the positive outcome ranges are for each of the negotiating variables for your company. This brings us to another major point in this chapter. It is called Paul and Peter's Rule of One.

Paul and Peter's Rule of One

Paul and Peter's Rule of One, or just the Rule of One for short, is a very crucial point for you as a professional sales negotiator. What this rule tells us is that whenever there is only one negotiating variable in the sales negotiation, the seller must lose. Let's see why.

As you know, sales transactions always seem to have a strong price focus. If it didn't have a strong price focus, you might not need to be reading this book. So, let's say that the sale comes down to a single factor: price. And let us assume that the seller, in this case, has power in this transaction over the buyer due to buyer's time constraints associated with the transaction.

As we know from our discussions surrounding the concept of win/win, if we charge too high a price, based on our leverage, we will create a win/lose outcome and the buyer may look to get back at us in the next transaction. Worse yet, they may decide not to work with us any longer. So, even though we charged a high price, we actually create a loss for ourselves in the relatively near future.

And, what about if we make an artificial price concession just to keep the customer happy? (An artificial price concession is one that is not required in the negotiation). If we make the price concession, we will erode our sales margins, again creating a potential loss for us.

When you have only one negotiating variable, you are destined to lose. You lose if you concede (on price) because you erode your sales margins. You also lose if you do not concede because you damage your relationship with the customer.

The reason that we are in this position is because, by allowing the negotiation to come down to only one variable, we have created what is known as a zero sum game. In a zero sum game, there must be a winner and there must be a loser. Any gains by one party come at the expense of the other party.

The best way to depict a zero sum game is with the pie analogy. Imagine that you are sharing a pie with another person. The pie is small so that it can be comfortably eaten by two people but it is very delicious. Assume that the pie is so small that you start to argue over the size of your piece. As you can imagine, the larger your piece, the smaller the piece for the other person.

This is exactly what we want to avoid with Paul and Peter's Rule of One. Don't create a zero sum game in a sales negotiation—you'll always lose.

However, Paul and Peter's Rule of One has an additional implication. The rule also tells us that sales negotiation (and sales for that matter) is about expanding the pie. If you handle the negotiation in the manner that we prescribe in this book, you will not have to fight over your slice of the pie. Rather, you will focus your attention on expanding the size of the pie. In this way, you can have a larger piece and so can the customer.

This is what we mean when we talk about win/win sales negotiations. Our definition of win/win sales negotiation is not only creating a win for both the customer and the salesperson, but it also means expanding the overall size of the pie so that you can each have a larger slice.

In order to create a win/win outcome for you and for the customer, you must become adept at creating a solution and negotiating a solution that adds value both to the customer's business and your business as well.

To learn how to add value to a customer's business, you may want to read our book *Red-Hot Customers, How to Get Them, How to Keep Them* (Chandler House Press, 1999).

Much of your ability to create value in the sales negotiation process will be learned in our discussions around "synthesizing the deal." We briefly introduced this idea in Chapter 1 when we were reviewing our copy machine case study. There, the customer and the seller agreed on the other terms and conditions but the customer did not have the funds to purchase the equipment this quarter. As you may remember, the seller proposed deferred billing in order to synthesize and close the deal.

While this is admittedly a simple example of synthesizing the deal, it does illustrate the point quite well. And you may ask what value was created for the customer? The value created by deferred billing was to allow the customer to get started immediately on their underlying project. The equipment required may have been for a department that had to comply with a government regulation such as Sarbanes-Oxley in the United States. If the department did not comply with the government regulation in a timely manner, they would have to pay large fines as a result of their non-compliance.

So, even with this simple example, you can see that it is possible to add value into the customer's business through the sales negotiation process. This is typically done in the deal synthesis stage of the negotiation but may be done in other stages of the negotiation as well (such as when you ask the customer open-ended negotiation questions as we will discuss in Chapter 8).

How to Implement Paul and Peter's Rule of One

Earlier in this chapter we introduced the idea of listing the variables involved in a sales negotiation. The nine variables we included in our list above were the following:

1. Price

2. Payment terms

3. Contract volume

4. Contract duration

5. Delivery schedule

6. Product or service options

7. Post-sale service and support

8. Training

9. Other resources

It is important to create a list specific to your company, your industry, and your product set. Make sure your list is in the order of importance to your company.

In Figure 3-1, we have taken our list and placed the variables in order of importance to our sample company. You should also create and prioritize a list of the variables, or a decision-making matrix, for the customer based on your discussions with them. Let's call this one of the few "homework" assignments in this book.

Some of the questions you can ask in the early stages of the sales negotiation are:

- Can you tell me what's important to you in this negotiation?

- What are your goals and objectives in this negotiation?

- What do you value in a relationship with a company like ours?

Any of these questions, or all of them in combination, can be used to help you understand what the customer's decision-making matrix actually looks like.

Win/win negotiating is not about pummeling the other side. Rather it is about working collaboratively with the customer to create an outcome that is good for both parties. In Chapter 2, we recom-

FIGURE 3-1. HOW TO IMPLEMENT PAUL & PETER'S RULE OF ONE

Our Company	The Customer
1. Contract duration	1. Price
2. Contract volume	2. Delivery schedule
3. Payment terms	3. Product options
4. Price	4. Post-sale service and support
5. Delivery schedule	5. Training
6. Product options	6. Contract duration
7. Post-sale service and support	7. Contract volume
8. Training	8. Payment terms
9. Other resources	9. Other resources

mended that you draw and discuss the win/win matrix (Figure 2-1) with your customer in an attempt to get them to buy in to the collaborative process, which is part of creating a win/win outcome.

The purpose of asking any of the questions outlined above is to get the customer to help you understand their value system or decision-making matrix. If the customers share this information with you, that is great. However, even if they don't, you should have some idea of what your customer values based on your past workings with this customer and your overall experience in working with many customers in the same industry.

So, Figure 3-1 now outlines both your priorities in the negotiation and those of the customer. The first thing that should jump out at you is that there are differences in the order of the negotiating variables. And this is where you can use Paul and Peter's Rule of One to your advantage.

If you have taken the time to order the negotiating variables, you should be well positioned to make trade-offs. Honestly, it should come as no surprise to the experienced seller that the customer is always going to ask for a price concession as part of the sales negotiation. And, often this is the one item that is left to negotiate (exactly wrong, according to Paul and Peter's Rule of One). Normally, this would place you in a very difficult situation. However, we are well prepared! If you take a look at Figure 3-1, you can see that contract duration is most important to us. Looking at your list of priorities and theirs, you should consider in advance what kinds of concessions you could make while still making it a win/win.

You should be prepared for their asking for a price concession or for other concessions that we may need to make in the sales negotiation. This is not to say that we are advocating that you make concessions. You want to do as well as you can within the context of creating a win/win outcome. However, let's be honest. There will be instances where you will have to make concessions in order to close the deal.

And, there is nothing wrong with making concessions as long as you understand exactly what you are doing.

So, let us assume that we are ready to wrap up the negotiation and the customer asks for a price concession of say, 5 percent. There are several things that we can do at this point.

First, 5 percent is not really that unreasonable so we could simply concede. However, you would never want to do this. Conceding immediately will tell the customer that you will be ready to make small price concessions in all subsequent negotiations. (Yes, it is true that your customer will think this way. Ouch!)

Key Negotiating Tactic   Train your customer. Every action on our part in a sales negotiation trains the customer how to behave with us on all subsequent sales negotiations.

Thus, think through everything that you do in a sales negotiation. You certainly don't want to be trapped into future concessions.

Now we know that we don't want to make an immediate concession, even if it's small and well within our range, still creating a win/win outcome. So, if this is the case, what do we do? What we need to do is remember Paul and Peter's Rule of One and return our attention to Figure 3-1.

Figure 3-1 tells us that the most important item for us in the sales negotiation is contract duration. What this means is that if the customer asks us for a small price concession, what we should do is ask them for a commensurate increase in contract duration.

Key Negotiating Tactic   Whenever you have to make a concession, ask for something of equal or greater value.

Asking for something of equal or greater value does two things for you. It tells the customer that you are unwilling to make unilateral concessions. Rather, each time they ask for a concession, they will also have to give something up in return. In this way, you are "training the customer" properly for our next sales negotiation.

Second, you are getting something very valuable for you and your company. Aren't you glad you took the time to order the negotiating variables in order of importance to your company?

At this point, it is worth noting that ordering your negotiating variables should be done together with your entire sales team: the sales manager and all of the related sales personnel. This way, everyone will be using the same matrix and it will truly reflect the values of the company.

Key Negotiating Tactic   Never make something look or sound easy.

Remember that the customer is looking at how we behave to learn about our values for this negotiation and for subsequent negotiations. Let us assume that the 5 percent concession was something that really would not be a big deal for us.

So, the customer asks for the 5 percent and you say sure, that's easy. I can do that.

By acting this way, you have told the customer that there was still plenty of room to negotiate. While they may not take advantage of that in the current negotiation, it is something that the customer, if they are astute, will take advantage of in the next negotiation. By stating that you can easily deliver on the 5 percent, you have told the customer that you really could have gone farther without it becoming too hard for you.

An appropriate response would be to make a big deal of the concession, ask for something of equal or greater value in return and grudgingly concede to the 5 percent. You may even want to include your manager in the process by saying that this is something outside your scope of authority. By doing this, you are establishing a "Higher Authority," something that you can use to great advantage in the negotiating process. ("Higher authority" will be discussed in depth when we explore Negotiating Ploys and Tactics in Chapters 10 and 11.)

At this point, it is important to understand that you should not make something look easy and you should always ask for something of equal or greater value in return.

Asking for Something of Equal or Greater Value in Return

The ten simple words listed immediately above this sentence appear to be somewhat ordinary, but they will make you and your company untold incremental revenue and commissions over the course of a career.

Remember that each incremental dollar received as part of an effective sales negotiation drops right to your company's bottom line and gets added directly to your commission check. While it is hard to imagine that one dollar's worth of incremental revenue is better than another, incremental revenue associated with effective sales negotiations or effective value selling is especially sweet. The reason is that incremental revenue comes in without any associated cost attached and hence there is a 100 percent incremental profit margin associated with each of those dollars. Likewise, incremental revenue is achieved by you without an incremental time investment and as we all know, time is extremely important within the professional sales community. The salesperson who invests his or her time most wisely, will, in general, sell the most.

So, what does all of this mean to you?

Let us explain.

I'm sure we have all at one time or another arrived at an airport only to find that our confirmed reservation was given to another passenger. In other words, we have no seat on the flight. This puts us into a negotiating position of sorts and the airline usually offers us free airline tickets to compensate us for our difficulties.

Why does this strategy often work so well? The reason is because our value system differs from that of the airline.

The value to us of a free airline ticket is the retail or purchase price of the ticket. The incremental cost of the ticket to the airline is usually very little: they will have to serve an additional meal and there may be a little extra wear and tear on your seat, but these are truly minimal costs.

Yes, we acknowledge that there may also be an opportunity cost but we are assuming that most flights do not take place at 100 percent of capacity. In case you are not familiar with the idea of an opportunity cost, it refers to the lost revenue the airline would suffer if their flights were running at 100% of capacity and they allow you to take a seat on the plane at no charge. However, many flights do not run at 100%

of capacity, eliminating the opportunity cost associated with the free ticket.

In any event, it is the difference in value systems, the fact that the value to us of a free airline ticket is greatly in excess of the cost to the airline that makes this negotiating tactic work so well. This idea also applies to our sales negotiations.

For example, our company typically sells to larger, Fortune 500 organizations. If you have ever worked with a larger organization, you will learn that one of their key negotiating criteria is that a project, program, or purchase be concluded on budget. Being "on budget" will often be very high on the negotiating list of a large corporation and this is something that we learned to use in our corporate negotiation process.

Our company is relatively small in comparison, and one of the more important items to a company like ours is cash flow. So, getting paid in a timely manner ranks very high on our negotiating priority scale.

When we first started our company, we were unaware of the length of time it would take and the difficulty we could encounter in attempting to get paid by some of the larger corporations. In fact, in many instances, it was near impossible. So, with our accounts receivable balances growing and our company starved of cash, we came up with the idea to ask our corporate customers to "prepay" for our services.

When we first broached the topic with our sales organization, we were told that a large corporation would never prepay for services. However, this did not stop us from trying. And what we found was that our value system was different than that of the customer. In fact, many large corporate customers were very willing to pay in advance in return for the guarantee that their purchase would come in on budget.

There is a very valuable lesson to be learned in all of this. Because the customer's value system is often different than ours, it can be relatively easy to create a win/win outcome. And, in fact, in many instances as long as you are skilled, it is.

All you need to do is to create you own Figure 3-1.

As noted above, you can sit down with your colleagues and create your side of Figure 3-1. You are now halfway there. Then, you can ask the customer a simple question like, "What's important to you in this sales negotiation?" After you get them to answer, simply ask them to prioritize their answer. Then, you will have their side of Figure 3-1. Now, look for the differences and you will be well on your way to creating a win/win outcome.

Remember to always ask for something of equal or greater value in return. To execute on this strategy all you have to do in response to a concession (typically on price) requested by the customer is to start asking for concessions on items on the top of your list.

You could say something along the lines of "I can understand why you are asking for that. Let me take that back to my manager (Higher Authority). However, when I go back to her for permission to grant you this concession, she will want to know what we are getting in return. Do you think it is fair to ask for . . . ?" At this point, simply ask for the first item on your list.

If your first item does not work, move on to your second. And if your second item does not work, solicit the customer's help in resolving the item that you are to get in return. After all, they know their business better than you do.

Conclusion

In our opinion, one of the key concepts in this chapter was contained in Figure 3-1. This was called Paul and Peter's Rule of One. To avoid being stuck with a single issue (price) on the negotiating table, the Rule of One forces you to create and prioritize two sets of negotiation variables, yours and a buyer's. The homework assignment we gave you earlier in the chapter should serve as a hands-on introduction to the concept of *planning* for your sales negotiation. Planning is crucial to your success in all phases of the sales cycle and that is what we are going to discuss in the next chapter of this book.

CHAPTER 4

Planning for the Negotiation

Having participated in hundreds and thousands of negotiations over many years, and having observed and viewed thousands more in our roles as teachers and consultants, we can state this about effective sales negotiations with 100 percent certainty. Much of your success, or failure for that matter, takes place before the negotiation ever takes place! Let's see why.

Peter and I come from different parts of the world but when we sat down to collaborate on this book, it became exceedingly apparent that one of our big obstacles was how we were going to position the "P" topic. Of course, "P" stands for "Planning."

For some reason, sales professionals worldwide are averse to planning. It's as if this aversion was part and parcel of the salesperson's innermost being. However, planning is a key activity of any top-notch, high-performance sales professional. Both Peter and I weekly-plan, territory-plan, account-plan, and negotiation-plan. It is from our dedication to planning that we have learned that sales is a learned skill. Sales is not an art form as many would claim; it is the "science" we mentioned in our opening chapter.

We have all heard people refer to a great salesperson as "having the gift of gab," but in fact, the gift of gab has very little if anything to do with selling success. Selling success depends on willingness to do the hard work of planning.

Salespeople protest the idea of planning of any sort. The protest often takes the following form: "Of course I want to plan. However, don't you (their manager) want me to service my existing accounts first?" The implication of this statement is that if you take the time to plan, you cannot possibly service your existing accounts.

We can look at this statement objectively and see that it makes absolutely no sense at all. If truth be told, we believe that if you *don't* take the time to plan, you cannot possibly service your existing accounts, much less get new ones.

Think of sales in terms of an athletic event. We said in Chapter 2 that there are three Olympic events in sales: the prospecting call to gain the appointment, the face-to-face meeting to discover the customer's needs, and the negotiation to close the sale. With these three Olympic events, don't you think that some preparation is in order? We do.

Your Negotiation Planner

Your "Negotiation Planner" is presented in Figure 4-1. What we intend to do in Figure 4-1 is to introduce a four-step negotiation planning process. The four steps of our process follow:

1. Prepare a list of the issues or items to be negotiated.

2. Prioritize the issues both in order of importance to us and in order of perceived importance to the customer.

3. Establish a "settlement range" for *each* significant item to be negotiated.

4. Select and prepare your strategies and tactics, including your negotiation discovery questions.

Please note that items one and two above will be discussed in depth in this chapter. Items three and four will only be referenced in

FIGURE 4-1. RED-HOT SALES NEGOTIATIONS™ NEGOTIATING MODEL

What Are the Issues?	Issues	Us	Them
	Price		
	Payment Terms		
	Contract Volume		
	Length of Agreement		
	Delivery Schedule		
	Product/Service Options		
	Post Sale Service and Support		
	Training		
	Resources		

Settlement Range	Us	Them	Settlement Range
Maximum			
Supportable			*Deal Breaker*
Really Asking			*Most Acceptable*
Minimum Acceptable			*Really Offering*
Deal Breaker			*Minimum Supportable*

Questions	Notes

What are your goals and objectives in the negotiation?

What's your future direction?

Please describe your decision-making process:
  • Time frames
  • Budgets
  • Parties

What's important to you in a relationship with a company like ours?

Is there anything else I need to know to successfully conclude this negotiation?

Strategies and Tactics	Yes/No

Higher Authority
Nibbles
Humble and Helpless
Straw Man
First Offer
Financial Justification

Notes:

this chapter and discussed in depth in subsequent chapters of the book.

Step #1: Prepare a List of Issues or Items to Be Negotiated

In Chapter 3, we had an in-depth discussion about Paul and Peter's Rule of One. There, we suggested that any time a negotiation comes down to one item—and that item is almost invariably price—the salesperson must lose.

What we learned is that we create a zero sum game or a negotiation in which the size of the pie to be divided among the parties is fixed. If the size of the pie is fixed, then there must be a winner and there must be a loser. In sales negotiations, we are usually the loser because we must make a price concession in order to maintain the integrity of the relationship. As a result, the customer gets a bigger piece of the pie and we get a smaller piece of the pie.

The whole purpose of introducing Paul and Peter's Rule of One was to prepare you for the concept of negotiation planning.

The first step in the negotiation planning process is to prepare a list of items to be negotiated. One of the things that we have learned over the years is that there are really only a fixed number of outcomes in the sales process.

If you were to take one of our basic selling skills programs, where we discuss the topic of overcoming objections, what you would learn is that there are really only four objections in the sales process. This is true irrespective of what you sell and irrespective of what part of the world that you do business in.

The four types of objections are:

1. Price ("Your price is too high.").

2. Competition ("We are working with one of your competitors.").

3. Will it work ("If I buy from you, will the implementation of your product, service, or solution be successful in my business?").

4. Not now (Typically this is a telephone prospecting objection where the party on the other side of the phone, the prospect, tells you that he or she is not prepared to meet with you now for a variety of reasons, including no current need, no budget, or no interest.).

The existence of only a limited number of objections that you can encounter in the sales process makes it quite a bit easier for us, the sales professional, to prepare.

The same is true in sales negotiations. How many variables can there be in the sales negotiations process? We suggest that it will only take you a few negotiations to realize that it will be quite easy for you to compile a list of the typical issues or items to negotiate in sales negotiations in your field.

If you take a look at Figure 4-1, you will see that we have provided you with a list of typical negotiation variables. These include:

- Price.
- Payment terms.
- Contract volume.
- Contract duration.
- Delivery or implementation schedule.
- Product or service options (If you were to think of a car, it would be negotiating items such as cloth seats [less expensive] versus leather seats [more expensive] or regular radio (AM and FM) alone or including satellite radio [a more expensive option.]).
- Post-sale service and support.
- Training.
- Other resources (i.e., what special resources will you provide to the customer in connection with their order? Special resources

could be something like access to your testing laboratory so that they can test a potential new application in your lab prior to implementation in the field. If you didn't provide them with lab access, they would either have to maintain a lab on their own or go out and rent one for a particular application.).

The goal here is to create a comprehensive list of negotiating variables that affect your sales negotiations. As we mentioned above, it should not be particularly hard to do this. Rather, you should be able to easily accomplish this by simply keeping track of the negotiation variables in your next three sales negotiations. If you do this, you will have a fairly comprehensive list of negotiation variables that impact your sales negotiations.

The value in doing this is that you will start to see a pattern in the items that you negotiate. You will learn that negotiations are not random events. Rather, negotiations are actually quite repetitive and you can gain a very significant advantage over the other side simply by preparing yourself.

Before we move on to the second step in the negotiation process, we need to make one more point. You do not need to worry if you prepare a list of five negotiation variables and you prepare for the negotiation on this basis and then a new negotiation variable, one that you haven't encountered before, or that you thought irrelevant to this buyer, enters the sales negotiation.

Something like this can always happen. You don't have to worry about it. No matter how much you plan, something unanticipated can always arise. The key is simply to learn from your experience.

What we recommend is that you pay special attention to this new negotiating point. Has it come up in other negotiations or not? If this is a once-in-a-lifetime experience, don't worry about it. Simply realize that you cannot possibly plan for every possible contingency and do the best you can.

However, if this new variable comes up again and again, we simply need to add this new item to our list of recurring negotiating variables and prepare for it on a prospective basis. If something new enters the negotiation process, it is OK. What is not OK is to not learn from your experience.

So at this point, you should have a fairly comprehensive list of negotiation variables customized specifically to your sales negotiations. There should probably be no more than five key elements of your sales negotiations; certainly no more than ten. You cannot afford to get too detail-oriented or you will run the risk of losing focus on what you are trying to accomplish (to create a win/win outcome) and you will spend all of your energies on maintaining a list of negotiating variables.

Remember the 80/20 rule. It tells you that 80 percent of your sales will come from 20 percent of your customers. However, the 80/20 rule applies to almost everything in life and in business. In our sales negotiations, 20 percent of the negotiating variables will impact 80 percent of the (win/win) outcomes, so it is a good idea to make your list of negotiating variables and then separate the list into two components: Those with high impact on the outcome and those with lesser impact on the outcome. Obviously, we will want to focus on the high-impact negotiating variables in our planning efforts.

This is not to imply that the lower-impact negotiating variables are not important. They are. They may be the items that allow us to move back and forth over the win/win threshold. They are also very useful in one particular negotiating tactic, an extremely powerful one called "Straw Man," which we discuss in Chapters 10 and 11. For now, we want to point out that the lower-impact negotiating variables still have an important use for us in the actual sales negotiation.

Step #2: Prioritize the Issues

When we talk about prioritizing the issues we are referring to the mission-critical issues identified in the preceding section. And, it is important to note that we must do this prioritization both in order of importance to *us* and in perceived order of importance to the *customer*.

How to Determine the Customer's Priorities

In the context of a typical sales negotiation we always recommend that the seller determine what the customer's objectives are in the sales negotiation. The reason we ask questions to this end is because it will help us in the planning of our negotiation strategy. If we know what their objectives are, then we can use that in a positive way to create a win/win outcome.

So, one important recommendation that we can make at this stage is to always come to the negotiating table with a prepared list of open-ended questions in much the same way as you would in a sales discovery session. One of your prepared questions ought to be, "Can you tell me what your objectives are in this sales negotiation?" Another great question to ask, as a follow-up to the question above is, "Can you help me prioritize your objectives?"

We realize that in some cultures, the negotiation protocol and customs will not allow for the asking of questions along these lines. However, in other cultures, a typical customer will not have a problem answering these questions. This type of customer will understand that you are asking these questions in the context of creating a win/win outcome. The more information they provide to you, the seller, the easier it will be for you to create this win/win outcome.

But whether you believe that your culture will allow you to ask questions like this is not the point. Our feeling is that you have nothing to lose. The worst that can happen is the customer will tell you that they are not going to answer questions. And then you can move on. But, at least you tried.

Obviously, if you gather this sort of information, it should be carefully stored in your company's Customer Relationship Management (CRM) system or in a manual account planning document. Either way, this is valuable information and you will want it the next time you engage with this customer in a sales negotiation.

But what if the customer will not openly share this information with you? You can still gather this information based on your observations of this and other customers. Furthermore, you may want to try to gather some of this information during the sales process and prior to the negotiation when the customer may not be so guarded.

In any event, it is important that you start to understand what it is that the customer values in a sales negotiation so that you can more effectively plan your negotiation. One item that will almost invariably be high on their list is price. You can count on the customer asking for a price concession in each and every sales negotiation.

Before we move on, there is one more important point that we must make. We always teach that every sales negotiation tells the customer how to negotiate with us in the next sales negotiation. So, if the negotiation is essentially over and the customer asks for one additional concession from us (called a "nibble") *and* we make the concession believing that it is not important based on its magnitude, the customer will learn that they can always "nibble" at the end of the sales negotiation. (We will learn much more about nibbles in Chapter 10.)

A good counter to a nibble on the part of the customer is to nibble back in return and this can be easily done with your prioritized list of negotiating variables.

An Important Point About Our Priorities

Just as it is important to know the customer's priorities, it is important that you understand your own, or your company's priorities. And this is not an exercise that you should do at the point of sale. This is something that you should think through long before every sales negotiation.

Ordinarily, this should be done on a company or team basis. Our priorities should not be individual priorities. Rather they should reflect the value of the company. This way, if you have to make a concession, you can get the single most valuable item in return.

So, let's say that you have made a valid attempt to prioritize the negotiation variables on the part of the customer. And, let's say that you have also worked with others in your company to make a similar prioritization on our side. There are two important things that you can do with this information.

The first thing that you can do is be prepared when the customer asks for a price concession.

We *never* advocate making a price concession but we do acknowledge that there will be many a time when even the best value seller and the best sales negotiator will have to make a price concession. Sometimes, we have to make these concessions just to make the customer happy and to maintain the integrity of the relationship.

So, when the customer asks for a price concession, we can at least ask for the single most important thing in return for us. If we have to make the price concession, maybe we can increase the contract size, the contract duration, or shorten the payment terms. All of these would be important to most selling companies. Which items is most important to your company will, of course come from your prioritized list of negotiating variables.

The second thing we can do is use our list to help us when the customer "nibbles" at the end of a deal as we briefly alluded to above. When they catch you just before you leave their office and they tell you about their "one more thing". You can say "I'm glad you brought that up! There was one more thing that I wanted to discuss with you as well". You, of course, were not going to bring this additional item up but as long as the customer is nibbling, we should nibble as well. This will get us a nibble of equal or greater value in return and it will tell the customer that they should not nibble on agreements with you once they are settled.

The most important thing that you should be looking for in this stage of the planning process are differences; differences in the way you prioritize the list and in the way the customer prioritizes the list. As we will learn, these differences will prove to be very useful when it comes time to create that win/win outcome that we have talked about so extensively in this book.

Conclusion

We learned in this chapter that there are a few key negotiating variables that impact each and every sales negotiation. These variables are listed both in this chapter and in Figure 4-1. When considering these variables it is important to rank them from both our perspective and the perspective of the customer. This way, we can effectively guide the customer to a win/win outcome in the sales negotiations.

In the next chapter, we are going to continue to look at the sales negotiations planning process and discuss some high-impact planning strategies.

CHAPTER 5

High-Impact Sales Planning Strategies

Let's continue our discussion of planning by learning what we call "high-impact" planning strategies. It has been our experience that sales negotiations are won and lost in the planning stages.

By way of examples one of my clients ran an energy company. They sold electricity. My client was negotiating with a major bank, one of the largest worldwide. My client was one of two finalists with whom the bank was negotiating; the other was Enron.

While negotiating against Enron might not seem that intimidating today, at the time they were one of the most successful companies around. They were certainly the dominant player in the energy market-place, feared by all who entered their playground.

So, if it wasn't enough to negotiate with one of the largest banks in the world, they also had to compete against Enron. So, what did they do? They called us in to help them negotiate and much to their surprise our first step was to create a "war room" so that we could plan out every aspect of the sales negotiation. We helped them gather all of the company executives into the room, from the CEO and the Vice President of Sales all the way down to the account executive on the account.

And, we pulled out Figure 5-1, our trusty planning tool. This is the same tool we presented to you in Chapter 4. We reproduce it here for your convenience. To entice you to read on, I will tell you that we were able to win a $41 million dollar contract at a $15 million dollar premium over Enron.

Our success was attributed to two factors: great value selling, and Figure 5-1. We had planned for every possible contingency and we were ready when we got into the final stages of the negotiation.

Your Negotiating Planning Process

In order to reproduce the success we had in the negotiation above, we need a process. A process is nothing more than a series of steps that can be followed from one sales negotiation to the next, by one salesperson or another, in order to produce consistently good results.

As we have already learned, our negotiation planning process has four steps:

1. List the issues.
2. Prioritize the issues.
3. Establish a settlement range.
4. Develop strategies and tactics.

We have already discussed the first two steps in the prior chapter, so let's move directly to our discussion of "settlement range."

What Is a Settlement Range?

The notion of a settlement range is a very powerful concept for the professional sales negotiator. In fact, the settlement range is where most deals will be won and lost. The settlement range has four components. In fact, the seller and the buyer each have their own four components. Let's start with the four elements of the seller's Settlement Range, as listed in Figure 5-1:

FIGURE 5-1. RED-HOT SALES NEGOTIATIONS™ NEGOTIATING MODEL

What Are the Issues?	Issues	Us	Them
	Price		
	Payment Terms		
	Contract Volume		
	Length of Agreement		
	Delivery Schedule		
	Product/Service Options		
	Post Sale Service and Support		
	Training		
	Resources		

Settlement Range	Us	Them	Settlement Range
Maximum			
Supportable			Deal Breaker
Really Asking			Most Acceptable
Minimum Acceptable			Really Offering
Deal Breaker			Minimum Supportable

Questions	Notes

What are your goals and objectives in the negotiation?

What's your future direction?

Please describe your decision-making process:
- Time frames
- Budgets
- Parties

What's important to you in a relationship with a company like ours?

Is there anything else I need to know to successfully conclude this negotiation?

Strategies and Tactics	Yes/No

Higher Authority
Nibbles
Humble and Helpless
Straw Man
First Offer
Financial Justification

Notes:

1. What is your Maximum Supportable Position?

2. What are you Really Asking?

3. What is your Least Acceptable Position?

4. What is your Deal Breaker?

Before we define each of these items, it is extremely important to note that price is not the only issue. You should be thinking about *each* of the negotiation variables listed in the first step of our four-step negotiation planning process. To only think of price will limit your planning efforts and will also serve to place you in a weak negotiating position. If you think only of price, you will have violated one of the most fundamental tenets of successful sales negotiations: Paul and Peter's Rule of One. Any time the sales negotiation comes down to one item, the salesperson most lose. Our job as professional sales negotiators is to expand the discussion. Our counterparts will always be trying to contract the negotiation. Their goal is to get the sales negotiation down to one variable, price, and if they succeed, they will almost invariably win. Our job, once we expand the discussion to several crucial variables, is also to *keep* the discussion expanded!

So, let's look at these four elements of the seller's "settlement range," one at a time.

The Maximum Supportable Position

With all of your negotiating variables in mind, your "Maximum Supportable Position" is the most that you can ask without losing your credibility at the negotiating table. If we were referring to price, you could say that the Maximum Supportable Position is the list price of your product or service. Or, if it were tradition in your industry to have a list price but offer the customer a 10 percent discount from the list price as the starting point of your negotiation, then the Maximum Supportable Position would be list price minus the 10 percent customary discount offered to all in the industry.

Length of agreement would be another good negotiating variable to look at for purposes of our discussion of this point. Let us assume that a one-year contract is normal in your industry when a customer selects your company as their provider of the product or service that you sell. However, let us also assume that it is possible to negotiate eighteen-month agreements and it is also possible to negotiate twenty-four-month agreements. Anything more would be considered far out of the norm in the industry. In this case, you could argue that your Maximum Supportable Position might be eighteen months if this were your first contract with the customer and twenty-four months if you have been working with the customer for quite some time.

So, our Maximum Supportable Position is the most that we could ask as a seller without losing our credibility in the eyes of the customer.

What Are You Really Asking?

The next element of our settlement range is "what are we really asking for?" What are we really asking for refers to the fact that we will likely settle the negotiation at an amount less than the Maximum Supportable Position. So, let us assume that your Maximum Supportable Position was the list price of your product; however, if you were to look at historical sales results at your company you would see that the average selling price at the company might be list price less a 30 percent discount. Since this is the average selling price at the company, you, and your management, would likely be very happy if you sold your product or service at a price equal to or near the list price minus 30 percent. So, you could say that what you are "really asking" is the amount that you could leave the negotiating table with and feel pretty good about what you accomplished.

Looking at another one of our negotiating variables, length of the contract, you could suggest that the amount you are really asking for is eighteen months if this is an old customer of yours and twelve months if this is a new customer.

Again, what you are really asking for is an amount that you could feel pretty good about when you leave the negotiating table. Anything above that amount would make you feel great because you probably would have done a really good job in the sales negotiation. Anything less than what you are really asking for brings us to our next negotiating variable, the Least Acceptable Position.

The Least Acceptable Position

The Least Acceptable Position is known in negotiating circles as your "bottom line". It is the line that you cannot cross if you want to maintain a win/win relationship.

Returning to our examples, the Least Acceptable Position with respect to price might be a selling price equal to a 10 percent gross margin on the cost (to you) of your product or service.

"Gross margin" typically refers to the direct costs of producing your product. It is essentially the cost to your company of getting a product or service ready for delivery to a customer. Gross margin is more typically associated with a product sale than a service sale but that detail is not important in this discussion.

So, assume that it costs your company an amount equal to 40 percent of your list price to build your product and get it ready for sale to the customer. Let us also assume that your company requires a minimum of 10 percent above that amount in order to have a barely profitable sale. In this case, your Minimum Acceptable Position is 50 percent of your list price because this is the amount that your company has decided is the dividing line between a profitable and unprofitable sale.

In our case, we have already acknowledged that a 30 percent discount is fairly common in the business so we said that this is our Really Asking price. Now you have just learned that you can discount above 30 percent by going to 40 percent discounts and even 50 percent discounts before your company would actually want to walk away from the sale. So, a 50 percent discount would be the Least Acceptable Position in this circumstance. Anything more than a 50 percent discount would put your company in a position where it is losing money on the sale and that is almost always to be avoided.

We will acknowledge that there are instances when a company

might want to sell a product at a loss, but again, that is not a discussion for this book. For our purposes, we need to have a bottom line if we are to be effective in sales negotiations. Our bottom line in this example is a 50 percent discount and it is what we are calling our "least acceptable position."

The Least Acceptable Position is the amount below which you cross from a win/win outcome to a win/lose outcome. In this case, the win refers to the customer and the loss is for us.

Let's take a look at the second example that we have been using, contract duration. We've said that our Maximum Supportable was a two-year or eighteen-month agreement depending upon our prior relationship with the customer. We also assumed that what we are really asking was also a function of the prior relationship with the customer; eighteen months in the case of a recurring customer and one year in the case of a new customer. Our Least Acceptable Position might be six months. Why six months? Because anything less would not allow our company to recoup the start-up costs associated with any new type of relationship, whether it is a totally new customer or simply a new product or service for an existing customer.

Another reason you might insist on at least six months is that there is always a learning curve when you are doing something new. Your company needs enough time to learn what it needs to do and to get into a smooth and consistent delivery mode. (Please note that we're not implying that the minimum length of an agreement ought to be six months. We used that number for illustration purposes in this chapter.)

So, for our second negotiating variable, contract duration, we are assuming that our Least Acceptable would be a six-month contract.

Now that we have defined our Maximum Supportable Position, our Really Asking, and our Least Acceptable Position, we are ready to look at the fourth element of our settlement range: the "Deal Breaker."

The Deal Breaker

Theoretically, the Deal Breaker is the next unit of measure below the Least Acceptable Position. So if our Least Acceptable Position was a

50 percent discount on prices and this equates to a price of $500 for one unit of the product or service you are selling, then the Deal Breaker would be a price of $499. Looking at our second negotiating variable, we said that the Least Acceptable Position for contract duration was six months. If this is the case, then the Deal Breaker would be five months and twenty-nine days.

When we teach our seminars on this topic, we often get into a debate about the value of one dollar or the value of one day, using our two examples. The point that we are trying to make is that there is some point at which you need to walk away from a negotiation. There *is* such a thing as a bad deal. So, it is not the one dollar that we are talking about, it is the cumulative impact of all of the dollars that we have chosen to give away. Likewise, it is not the one day; it is the cumulative impact of all of the days that we have chosen to concede.

There is an old saying that's relevant here: "That was the straw that broke the camel's back." Now, we all know that one straw does not break a camel's back. However, if you put enough straws in the load, there will be one straw that crosses the border of tolerance. There will actually be the one straw that does break the camel's back and that is what we are referring to here. There is some point at which your price is too low and it does not make business sense for your company to proceed. There is some point where the contract is too short and it does not make sense for your company to proceed. The Deal Breaker concept tries to capture that point.

What would take place if the Deal Breaker did *not* "break" the deal? If your Least Acceptable Position is in fact $500 and your Deal Breaker is $499, here's what happens if you take the position that the difference between the two amounts is only $1 and therefore you should concede.

Well, now you are at a Least Acceptable Position of $499. If this is the case, then what is your Deal Breaker? Because you made the concession, your Deal Breaker now becomes $498 and you are in the same position as you were before. Why would you want to lose business for $1? Using the same logic, you wouldn't. So, now you will make a second concession and your Least Acceptable Position becomes $498 and your Deal Breaker becomes $497.

You see where this is heading. If there is no Deal Breaker, then there is no such thing as a "bad deal." And if there is no such thing as a bad deal, this suggests that we can sell at any price, even a loss, to close a sale—and we all know that this is simply not true. So, your Deal Breaker is the point at which you *must* walk away from the negotiating table.

But there is one more key point to make before moving away from the topic of Deal Breaker. If you find yourself at your Least Acceptable Position and are contemplating *not* walking away, if you are thinking of taking that rash next step and moving into the realm of a win/lose outcome, you must be pretty desperate. The major reason this step is taken is because of a lack of a pipeline. In case you are not familiar with the term "pipeline" or "sales pipeline", let us define it for you.

What Is Your Sales Pipeline?

Your sales pipeline is that amount of active opportunities that you have in your sales funnel to help you meet your sales goals for the current sales period. So, let us assume that you are starting the fourth quarter of the year. And, let us also assume that you need $250,000 in sales to close during the fourth quarter in order to reach your sales goal for the year.

You would probably have a number of different opportunities in your sales funnel that you would be counting on to help you reach your sales goal. Let us assume that you have five opportunities that you are working on, with a total value of $500,000. This, then, would be your sales pipeline. Your sales pipeline is the sum of all of the opportunities that you are currently working on that you would expect to close in the current sales period in order for you to reach your sales goals.

Just as a pointer, you should always try to have at least three to four times your sales goal in your sales pipeline. What we are suggesting is that if you hope to reach your sales goal on a consistent basis, quarter in and quarter out, you should have three to four times your sales goal in your sales pipeline. With a goal of $250,000, your pipeline coverage should be in the $750,000 to $1,000,000 range. This is not to imply that you will not reach your sales goals if you have less in your sales pipeline. You may, but you are leaving too much to chance if you don't consistently plan in this manner.

Having less than three times your sales goal in your sales pipeline will generally force you to make poor decisions, such as steep discounting, in order to expedite the sale and reach your goal in the current period. Discounting, as we know, is a long-term decision and will create a problem for you in every succeeding quarter because you will always be moving deals from the next quarter to the current quarter by discounting in order to continually support your less-than-adequate sales pipeline coverage.

Let us show you a real case study of what can happen when you have less-than-adequate pipeline coverage. Pipeline coverage is simply the value of your sales pipeline divided by the value of your sales goal. As you know, we have recommended that this be in the three to four range, if not higher.

Back to the Value of a Full Pipeline

Not too long ago, our company was asked to train the North American sales organization of a company in our program, Red-Hot Sales Negotiations™. It was a technology company and competition was stiff, especially as quarter end approached. In fact, the customer would often wait until quarter end to start their negotiation so that the sales person would have to lower their price in order to get the sale into the quarter that was closing. Remember that our client was a publicly held corporation.

We went on to train the sales team and we learned something very important. Competition was a big issue in their business and so was the close of a quarter. Wall Street also played a role in the negotiation because better sales numbers meant a higher stock price.

However, after working with the company for a short period of time, we learned something very interesting. Their issue wasn't a negotiating issue. They were skilled negotiators, which is not to say that a program like ours wouldn't help. It did. However, their main issue was not negotiation prowess: it was pipeline. Actually it was a lack of pipeline that was causing the most difficulties at the company.

At the end of a quarter, most of their sellers would be below their goal and they were in the very difficult position of having to meet their goal, no matter what. And they did meet the goal, but at the expense of margin.

We want to go on record now as telling you that what you learn in this book will be incredibly helpful to you. Both of us reflect on the difference in our skills after we read our first negotiating book. However, we also want to be perfectly clear that the *single best negotiating strategy in the world, bar none, is that of having a full sales pipeline.*

A full sales pipeline gives you options. And options mean that you can afford to walk away from a deal that is not good for you or for your company. A full pipeline will give you the confidence you need to close a *win/win* deal—or not close it at all. Everything in this book will work wonders for you, but they will work a whole lot better if you have a full pipeline.

We cannot overemphasize the importance pipeline plays in the sales negotiation process. Without a full pipeline, you *must* close the deals that you have in order to make your sales goals for the quarter or the year. The lack of a pipeline leads to unnecessary concessions on the part of the sales person.

The concept of a Deal Breaker is a very powerful concept—but only if you are in fact free to walk away from a win/lose outcome. Don't lose its benefit because you have not focused on the basics of the sales process, that of filling your sales pipeline!

Making a Commitment

Before we move on to the next point, we are going to give you a very practical negotiating tip. What we do, in preparing for a negotiation, is to produce something like what you see in Figure 5-2.

Key Negotiating Tactic   Document your Least Acceptable Position and Deal Breaker during the planning process.

Once you have completed your planning and are ready to go to the negotiating meeting, give your Least Acceptable Position and Deal

	Seller	Buyer
FIGURE 5-2. SETTLEMENT RANGE FOR PRICE SELLER'S PERSPECTIVE		
Maximum Supportable Position	1,000	Deal Breaker
Really Asking	700	Most Acceptable Agreement
Least Acceptable Position	500	Really Offering
Deal Breaker	499	Minimum Supportable Position

Breaker amounts to a colleague. This could be a friend at work, another sales buddy preferably, or it could be your manager. Either way, document your Least Acceptable Position and Deal Breaker amounts and give it to a trusted colleague.

What this forces you to do is to make a commitment as to the outcome. Since you are making a commitment and the commitment is to a trusted colleague or manager, you will fight very hard at the negotiating table to honor the commitment you made to your company.

When you return from the negotiation, your colleague or manager will want to know how you did. Imagine having to tell them that you violated every commitment that you made to them. That would be terrible. So, the act of documenting your plan and then making a firm commitment to your plan can be a very powerful ally at the sales negotiating table.

The Customer's Settlement Range

When you take a look at Figure 5-2, you will note that the column marked "Buyer" is empty. So let's move on to Figure 5-3, where that column has been filled in, and take a look at the customer's side of the equation.

The first thing you will notice is that the titles of the categories are not the same, and they are not in the same order—in fact, they appear in opposite order.

FIGURE 5-3. SETTLEMENT RANGE FOR PRICE SELLER'S PERSPECTIVE, AND NOW ADDING THE BUYER'S PERSPECTIVE

	Seller	Buyer	
Maximum Supportable Position	1,000	801	Deal Breaker
Really Asking	700	800	Most Acceptable Agreement
Least Acceptable Position	500	600	Really Offering
Deal Breaker	499	500	Minimum Supportable Position

1. Deal Breaker

2. Most Acceptable Agreement

3. Really Offering

4. Minimum Supportable Position

As a seller, you start the negotiation with a high selling price and then you move to progressively lower selling prices. So, the Maximum Supportable Position is the highest price in the table, and the Really Asking price is somewhat lower than the Maximum Supportable Position. Beneath the Really Asking, the Least Acceptable Position is at an even lower price point, and finally, the Deal Breaker is the lowest price in the seller's table.

The customer's table works just the opposite.

If you look at the customer's table, the best place to start is at the bottom. Their starting point for the negotiation is the *Minimum Supportable Position*, which is just like our Maximum Supportable Position with the exception that it shows up at the opposite end of the table. If you recall, our Maximum Supportable Position was the most that we could ask without losing credibility with the customer. If we asked more, the negotiation would immediately end. The customer would not consider you a realistic negotiation partner.

Just like we have boundaries placed upon us, so does the customer. They are bound by the same test of reasonableness as we are.

We have already started with the assumption that the list price of our product or service is $1,000. For purposes of our discussion, let us assume that we are selling a product. There is a general rule in accounting that says that you should set the list price of your product at double its manufacturing cost. So, in our example, our product has a list price of $1,000. What this means is that a customer can readily assume that our cost of manufacturing or producing our product is $500. (This discussion is not meant to imply that all companies have a gross margin of 50 percent of the list price of their product. I am just using this as an example of how the customer might think in our sample negotiation.)

So the customer's Minimum Supportable Position is going to be somewhere along the lines of $500, based on our list price of $1,000 and their assumption that our gross margin percentage is 50 percent.

As we mentioned earlier, a company's gross margin percentage is equal to all of the direct manufacturing costs of producing the product, divided by, in this case, the list price of the product. Even the customer knows that we cannot sell our products and services at a loss! So, they can do a quick calculation and determine that if they offer less than $500, you will not consider them a serious buyer for your product or service. Again, the negotiation would come to a quick and premature end. You would get up and leave.

So, buyer's Minimum Supportable Position is the least that the customer could offer to a seller without losing their credibility in the eyes of the seller.

Before we move on to the next point, please consider one more thing about the Minimum Supportable Position. The customer actually needs what we sell. That is the reason you are at the negotiating table. They must buy our product or service from someone. Because of the fact that they have a need on their part, they must be bound by the test of reasonableness. Their desire to get a deal done is no less than ours. We need their money but they need our product or service just as much!

Now, as we suggested above, the customer's portion of the table works just the opposite of ours. Since we started with the list price and worked down, they start at their Minimum Supportable Position and work up.

The next point in the customer's side of the table is "What are they Really Offering." Again, even the customer realizes that we must earn a profit. I know it may not seem like they do some of the time, but trust me, they do.

So, their Really Offering is very similar to our Really Asking.

The customer's Really Offering is the amount (more than the minimum supportable and less than the most acceptable) that would satisfy the customer's needs in the negotiation. This is the amount that the customer would really like to pay at the end of the sales negotiation. This is the customer's expectation of a satisfactory end result of the negotiation process. In our example in Figure 5-3, let us just assume that the customer will let us earn just a little bit of money. So, their Really Offering price could be $600 for purposes of continuing with our example.

Moving up the table, there is many an instance where we, the seller, actually have the upper hand in the negotiation process. For example, the customer could be under severe time pressure to get the product or service. Or, we could have a very strong track record of success with the customer, making it very difficult for them to switch to another company. Or, there could be a circumstance where the competition cannot deliver in the customer's required time frame. All of these could contribute to the customer paying more than they really wanted to in the sales negotiation.

To continue with our illustration, let us assume that the customer has a budget in place that would prohibit them from paying more than $800 per unit. This would mean that their Most Acceptable Agreement position would be $800.

The Most Acceptable Agreement is the most the customer could offer and still have a win/win outcome. In our example, it would not be possible for the customer to exceed their annual budget. Under these circumstances it would simply be impossible for the customer to pay more than $800.

The final point in the buyer's side of Figure 5-3 is the Deal Breaker. The customer's Deal Breaker is exactly the same as ours, but moving in the opposite direction. Their Deal Breaker is one unit of measure *above* their Most Acceptable Agreement. The reason I say one "unit of measure" is because in a sales negotiation, we don't want to just negotiate the price. Keep in mind Paul and Peter's Rule of One, which tells us that when a sales negotiation comes down to only one negotiating variable, say price, the salesperson must lose. By way of review, because this is an important point: if we concede, we obviously lose; if we don't concede, we damage the relationship and lose again. So, we never want to have just one negotiating variable. That is why we define the Deal Breaker by using the words unit of measure instead of dollar or other currency unit.

So, the Deal Breaker for the customer is one unit of measure above their Most Acceptable Agreement. In this case, the unit of measure is dollars and their Deal Breaker would be $801.

Some Key Points About the Settlement Range

Now that we have defined and reviewed each element of the settlement range, from the prospective of both the seller and the buyer, there are still a few other key points that we must consider. In order to review what we have accomplished, we are going to re-present Figure 5-1 as Figure 5-4. Figure 5-4 is our Negotiation Planner.

The steps in the sales negotiation planning process are:

1. *List the issues.* You can see the list of issues very clearly in Figure 5-4.

2. *Prioritize the issues.* If you look just to the right of the list of issues in Figure 5-4, you will see the space that we have allotted for your prioritizations. The goal here is to prioritize the negotiation issues in order of importance to you.

Then, you must also do your best to prioritize the issues in order of importance to the customer. While this is only an estimate, you should have a fairly good understanding of the customer's priorities if

FIGURE 5-4. RED-HOT SALES NEGOTIATIONS™ NEGOTIATING MODEL

What Are the Issues?	*Issues*	*Us*	*Them*
	Price		
	Payment Terms		
	Contract Volume		
	Length of Agreement		
	Delivery Schedule		
	Product/Service Options		
	Post Sale Service and Support		
	Training		
	Resources		

Settlement Range	*Us*	*Them*	*Settlement Range*
Maximum			
Supportable			*Deal Breaker*
Really Asking			*Most Acceptable*
Minimum Acceptable			*Really Offering*
Deal Breaker			*Minimum Supportable*

Questions	*Notes*

What are your goals and objectives in the negotiation?

What's your future direction?

Please describe your decision-making process:
- Time frames
- Budgets
- Parties

What's important to you in a relationship with a company like ours?

Is there anything else I need to know to successfully conclude this negotiation?

Strategies and Tactics	*Yes/No*

Higher Authority
Nibbles
Humble and Helpless
Straw Man
First Offer
Financial Justification

Notes:

you do a good job of asking good, open-ended questions during both the sales discovery and the negotiation discovery processes.

3. *The next step in our negotiation process is to establish the settlement ranges.* Here, we are going to recommend that you prepare a settlement range for the top three negotiating variables on each side of the table. So, you need to prepare a settlement range for our top three negotiating variables and for the top three negotiating variables of the customer. Some of these negotiating variables will probably overlap but at the most, you will have to prepare six sets of settlement ranges.

Obviously, preparing your settlement ranges must be measured against the size of your deal so for small deals, maybe you only prepare a settlement range for price. For moderate size deals, you prepare a settlement range for price and one other negotiating variable, and for your top deal, like the $41 million deal that we discussed at the beginning of the chapter, you would want to prepare all three negotiating variables on each side. In a case such as this, you may even want to prepare more. $41 million is a lot of money where I come from.

When we took the time to actually go through preparing a settlement range earlier in this chapter, we told you that the seller's settlement range would work down: We start with a high price and we are negotiated downward by the customer until we actually reach the deal price.

On the customer's side, it works just the opposite: They start at a low price and we negotiate them up until again, the deal price is reached.

There are times, however, when the settlement ranges get turned upside down. Let's take a look at the issue of payment terms.

In the case of payment terms, we, the sellers, would want shorter payment terms so that we could get our money faster. On the other hand, the customer would want to negotiate just the opposite. They would want to negotiate longer payment terms so that they could hold onto their money as long as possible. In this case, the table would look like that in Figure 5-5.

	Seller	Buyer	
Deal Breaker	46	60	Maximum Supportable Position
Most Acceptable Agreement	45	45	Really Asking
Really Offering	30	30	Least Acceptable Position
Minimum Supportable Position	15	29	Deal Breaker

FIGURE 5-5. SETTLEMENT RANGE FOR PAYMENT TERMS SELLER'S PERSPECTIVE AND BUYER'S PERSPECTIVE EXPRESSED IN DAYS

As you can see, the tables are flipped from the one that we studied in Figure 5-3. However, the principals are exactly the same.

There is one final point that we need to discuss on the topic of the settlement range.

Training the Customer

If you recall, in Chapter 3, we discussed the point that each action you take in a sales negotiation trains the customer on how to behave with you during the next negotiation.

This is why you must consider discounting as a sales and negotiation strategy. When you set a price at a 40 percent discount, just to establish an extreme example, the customer interprets this to mean that you can still earn a profit at a 40 percent discounted price point. This means that they will consider the 40 percent discount as the ceiling price for the next sales negotiation and will expect an even larger discount.

While it is possible to negotiate back up to lesser discounts by using sound value selling and negotiating techniques, it is a long and tedious process. The better option would be to sell value in the first instance and not have to offer such a significant discount.

Since each behavior that we exhibit in a negotiation trains the customer on how to behave with us in the next sales negotiation, we must literally consider everything that we do in a negotiation from the perspective of its implications on the customer's thought and behavior processes not just in this negotiation but in all the future ones.

In terms of settlement ranges, what this means is that you cannot just start at your Maximum Supportable Position and randomly move lower and lower until you reach your bottom line. Rather, you must *have a reason* for every movement in the settlement range.

This is tricky. Movements within the settlement range are complicated by the fact that any deal within the settlement range be a good deal for you. So, you must be careful not to confuse your satisfaction with your location within the settlement range and your desire to close the deal, with the need not to establish negative precedents for future negotiations.

Making Concessions

Let's start this section by first defining what we mean by a concession. A concession is any movement in a negotiating variable that would result in a lower value for us. As noted above, the movements can be both positive and negative depending on the negotiating variable that we are working with.

If we are working with price, a negative movement would be downward movement or a reduction in price. If, on the other hand, we are working with payment terms, a negative movement would be an increase in the payments terms. The longer the payment terms, the less valuable the deal becomes for us.

So, a concession can be either a positive movement as in the case of payment terms or a negative movement in the case of price. However, in either event, a concession results in a less valuable deal for us.

The next step in understanding concessions is to understand that there are better concessions and there are worse concessions. The better concessions are movements within your settlement range. Remember we concluded that any deal within your settlement deal is a good deal for you. So, if we were again working with price and our price settlement range is $100 to $80 per unit, any deal within this range is a good deal for you. Obviously, the closer we are to $100, the better the deal is for us and the closer we are to $80 the worse the deal becomes but it is still a good deal. Why? Because the outcome fell within our pre-defined settlement range.

The problem with movements within our settlement range is that while the deal is still a good deal for you, you can send some bad messages to the customer you are negotiating with. Continuing with this example, let us assume that you are at $90 on price and the customer tells you that they are willing to settle at $85. If you are like most of us, you may readily agree to this concession because it is still within the settlement range and it allows you to close the deal, hopefully in a win/win manner which is your major objective.

The point is if you tell the customer that their suggested price is not a problem, yes, you have closed the sale within your settlement range but you have also told the customer that the next time they negotiate with you they should try to push you even further because of the ease with which you made your concession.

Because the customer is always evaluating your every behavior in a sales negotiation, it is a good idea to always provide a reason for your movements within the settlement range. In other words, you should be framing your movements within the settlement range. This will remind the customer that your movement is strictly due to a unique set of circumstances that will not exist in the next negotiation. This will tell them that they will not be able to ask for concessions with great ease and that each concession that you make will be carefully evaluated in the context of a win/win outcome.

So, let's take a look at a few reasons for your movements within the settlement range. Common reasons for movements within the settlement range include:

- *Build a good relationship.* This might be used on your first order as long as it is made specifically clear that the discount is not an ongoing discount.

- *Volume discount.* Here, you are giving the customer a discount based on a specific and large sales volume. Again, you need to be very clear that the discount is related to the volume of the deal and will not apply on any future, smaller deals.

- *Beat the competition.* There may be instances where you are in a particularly competitive position. Suppose the incumbent at the account is one of your largest competitors and you are trying to penetrate the account. It is difficult to penetrate accounts because as the outsider you often do not have access to the information required to establish value and build a strong business case. By doing a one-time-only discount, you can get your foot in the door at the account and use that as an opportunity to build value for your second sale. Again, make sure you are very clear to the customer as to why you are giving the discount.

- *Discount on A if you buy B.* By adding a second product to the deal, you are increasing the overall deal size and you can often use this as a reason for movement within the settlement range as well. This obviously is very close to a volume discount because the overall size of the deal is increasing.

The second type of concession that you have to make is a true concession. A true concession is one where the movement will land you outside of your settlement range. Remember that this may move a deal from win/win to lose/win; a loss for us and a win for the customer. Because these types of concessions are technically more critical than the movements within your settlement range, we thought it would be a good idea to review a few good strategies to use when the customer makes a demand that may or will place you outside of your settlement range.

Concession Strategies

I. *Never accept the other party's first offer if their first offer falls outside of your settlement range.* Here, when the customer makes an offer, especially an offer that will place you outside of your settlement range, you can just act very surprised. You can even suggest that their offer is outside of what one would consider a reasonable offer. Do *not* make a counteroffer in a case like this. If you were to make a counteroffer you would be suggesting that their first offer actually has legitimacy. Instead, tell the customer that their first offer is truly unreasonable and that they must make a better or improved offer before you will respond. You can also remind the customer that their offer will not create a win/win outcome and they must make another, more reasonable offer before you will begin the negotiation process on this one point.

2. *Lower expectations by making small concessions.* Consider an example where you start at the high end of your settlement range. Using the example we have been using in this chapter where the settlement range extends from $100 to $80, let's say we start the negotiation at the high end of our settlement range at $95. This only represents a 5% discount from your list price and will probably not lie within the customer's settlement range. You will probably have to make additional concessions in order to create a win/win outcome. When the customer tells you that your price is too high, a good way to make your concessions at this point is to make them in relatively small amounts. A concession of $10 as your first concession would be relatively large in our example and it would also tell the customer that you still have room to move even more though we know that you really don't. A better concession might have been $2 or $3. This type of concession would tell the customer that you are nearing your bottom line, when in fact we can see that you still have a ways to go. Making small concessions like this will help your concessions still land within your settlement range after the negotiation is complete and you have closed the sale. What we have done by making small concessions in the beginning of the negotiation is to get the customer to lower their expectations by only making very small concessions on a particular point. This tells the customer that you are nearing the end of your settlement range and will not be able to make many additional concessions on this point.

3. *Make concessions slowly.* This point is very closely related to point two above and it is also very closely related to point four that follows. Make your concessions slowly as well as in small amounts. By

slowly, we mean let the customer request a concession multiple times. You could also try to defer a discussion on this topic to a later stage of the negotiation. By making your concessions slowly and in small amounts, you will also tell the customer that you are nearing the end of your settlement range and that they will need to conclude this portion of the sales negotiation.

4. *Make every concession seem important.* This point is related to the prior two points. In fact, they can be used with great impact if used together. You never want a concession to seem easy. That reduces and even minimizes the impact of the concession. When I hear a seller say, "Oh, we can do that. That is easy," I cringe. There should be no such thing as an easy concession as far as our customers ever know. This way, you will get full credit for every concession that you have to make. As opposed to the words above, you may try something like, "Hmm, let me think about that. (Pause.) I'm not sure if we can do that. We have never done that before but let me give it a try for you in the interest of getting to a win/win outcome and building our relationship."

5. *Defer concessions on matters important to you.* This point is fairly straightforward. If you practice the points we have suggested above, you will not be accepting the customer's initial offer because you will be posturing that it is unreasonable, you will not be responding to unreasonable offers, you will be making smaller and smaller concessions, you will be making your concessions slowly and thoughtfully and you will be making each concession seem important. By the time you have covered all of your less important issues, you will be able to turn to the customer and ask them to reflect on all of the difficult concessions that you have already made. By doing this, it will be easier to speed through the negotiating variables toward the end of the negotiation. The customer will be getting tired and will start to make their concessions faster and more frequently in order to conclude the negotiation. By deferring your important issues (and you know which they are because you have taken the time to prioritize them) you will have made a lot of concessions earlier in the negotiation but on issues that

are not that important to you. You can then argue, at this point, that you have made enough concessions and will not be able to create a win/win outcome if you make further, substantial careers.

6. *Don't make the first concession on an important issue.* Again, you should know what is important to you and what is not. Why? Because you have taken the time to prioritize your issues earlier in the planning process. You should try to refrain from making the first concession on an issue that is important to you. This would have the effect of starting the ball rolling in a negative direction for you.

7. *Get something in return for all concessions.* Our last point is something that we discuss again and again throughout this book so we won't go into an in-depth discussion here. Because we have taken the time to prioritize our negotiating variables and those of the customer, it should be relatively easy to get something valuable in return. Prioritizing the negotiating variables in order of importance to both us and the customer clearly gives us a tremendous advantage in the negotiating process.

Developing Strategies and Tactics

We have discussed three of the four steps in our negotiation planning process. The first step was to list the negotiating variables or issues in the negotiation. The second step was to prioritize the issues. We have seen in this chapter and others how important these two steps are.

The third step was to establish your settlement ranges and the fourth step is to plan your strategies and tactics. You should note that this is where most people *start* the negotiation. And they even start halfway through this final step.

We start our planning process at the beginning and, based on the years and years of negotiation experience that we have between the two of us as well as what we have observed about our clients, we can tell you that sales negotiations are won and lost long before you reach the negotiating table.

Your success as a professional sales negotiator will be determined by how well you prepare. This is no different than what would happen if you were a professional athlete; you prepare to win or you prepare to fail. In fact, if someone were to ask me how we won the $41 million deal discussed at the start of this chapter at a $15 million premium over a much larger and more powerful competitor and successfully negotiated with one of the worlds largest and most successful companies, I would answer in one word: planning.

The last step of the negotiation planning process is to plan your strategies and tactics, and this part actually has two substeps as well.

The first substep is to list the questions you are going to ask in the discovery phase of the negotiation. This occurs very early on in the negotiation process, and like many of the other points that we have made, is crucial to your success.

Just like you must discover a customer's needs early in the sales process, you must discover the customer's interests in the early phases of the negotiation process.

As in the sales discovery process, it is crucial that we ask the customer good, open-ended questions to learn about their interests and to prevent them from using some very powerful negotiating ploys. We are going to discuss this point in great detail in Chapter 8 of this book, so I will leave the in-depth analysis to that chapter.

The second major substep in the final phase of the negotiation planning process is to determine which negotiating ploys we are going to use and how we are going to use them. We must also try to figure out which negotiating ploys the customer is going to use and develop a strategy to counter them. You'll do a more detailed analysis of ploys in Chapters 11 and 12 of this book, so keep on reading.

So, the final step of the negotiating process is to plan your strategies and tactics and there are two components to this fourth and final step. The first part is to plan your negotiation discovery questions and the second part is to plan the implementation of your negotiating ploys as well as the counters to the customer's likely implementation ploys.

Most sellers and most customers start their negotiation planning, *if they plan at all*, with the second half of the final step. "What negotiating ploys am I going to use?" and "What might the customer have up their sleeve?" they may ask. But they avoid the hard work that will bring their sales negotiations to a satisfactory win/win conclusion.

What Happens When Your Settlement Ranges Do Not Overlap?

Believe it or not, we have left the most important point of this chapter for last. We have reproduced Figure 5-3 here for your convenience as Figure 5-6. If you take a look at the settlement ranges for both the customer and the seller, you should see that they overlap.

What this means is that it should be relatively easy to create a win/win outcome. Why? This overlap means that a win/win outcome for you is consistent with a win/win outcome for the buyer.

However, the problem in many sales negotiations is that the settlement ranges do *not* overlap. If you take a look at Figure 5-7, you'll see what we are talking about. Here, our Least Acceptable Position is $900 and the customer's Most Acceptable Agreement is $600. There

FIGURE 5-6. SETTLEMENT RANGE FOR PRICE SELLER'S PERSPECTIVE AND BUYER'S PERSPECTIVE (REPEATED)

	Seller	*Buyer*	
Maximum Supportable Position	1,000	801	Deal Breaker
Really Asking	700	800	Most Acceptable Agreement
Least Acceptable Position	500	600	Really Offering
Deal Breaker	499	500	Minimum Supportable Position

FIGURE 5-7. SETTLEMENT RANGE FOR PRICE SELLER'S PERSPECTIVE AND BUYER'S PERSPECTIVE SETTLEMENT RANGES DO NOT OVERLAP

	Seller	*Buyer*	
Maximum Supportable Position	1,000	601	Deal Breaker
Really Asking	950	600	Most Acceptable Agreement
Least Acceptable Position	900	550	Really Offering
Deal Breaker	899	500	Minimum Supportable Position

is a $300 difference between the minimum we are willing to accept and the maximum they are willing to pay. A situation like this is very common in the real world.

In Figure 5-6, our Least Acceptable Position is $500 and the customer's Most Acceptable Agreement is $800. That is what we mean when we say that the settlement ranges "overlap". If you remember that any deal within your settlement range is a good deal, by definition, than you can see that there is a range from $500 on the seller's side to $800 on the buyer's side within which to create a deal. As we said above, this should be relatively easy to do. We have a range of $300 within which to create a win/win outcome for both parties.

However, as we also noted above, this is not often the case in the real world. In the real world, we may come across a case where the settlement ranges do not overlap. As we see in Figure 5-7, our bottom line is $900 and their top line is $600. Instead of having a range of $300 to create a win/win outcome for both the buyer and the seller, we have a range of $300 that we must "make up" or account for.

We call this activity "synthesizing the deal."

As you may imagine, this is an absolutely crucial skill when you are negotiating in the real world. Most, if not all of your deals will require some element of synthesis.

In brief, our position is that it is the seller's responsibility to synthesize the deal. The buyer could simply go to another vendor and get the deal they are looking for. So, unless we synthesize the deal, we risk losing the deal when the settlement ranges do not overlap. We will show you how to do this in Chapter 6.

How to Synthesize a Deal

In the last chapter, we learned one of the most important lessons you will ever learn in sales negotiations. The lesson is that there will be many an instance where you will need to "synthesize the deal."

In Chapter 5, we learned about settlement ranges and told you that any deal within your settlement range was a good deal for you. The same is true of the customer. Any deal within their settlement range is a good deal for them.

This means that in order to create a win/win outcome, you need to create an outcome where the three top negotiating variables on each side actually fall within their respective settlement ranges.

If the settlement range of the seller and the settlement range of the buyer overlap or intersect, it's easy to create a win/win. The unfortunate thing in sales negotiations is that it is more likely that the settlement ranges will not overlap or intersect. Using our technical definitions from the prior chapter, this means that our Least Acceptable Position is actually *greater* than the buyer's Most Acceptable Agreement—that is, the lowest price we will accept is greater than the highest price the buyer will pay. In a case like this it's necessary to synthesize a deal.

In order to understand how to "synthesize a deal" using a real case study, consider the following condensed facts for a real selling situation:

Seller's Facts

1. An existing customer has just called you in for a meeting.

2. It is your understanding that the customer has been using your company, XYZ Company, for years and is reasonably happy with both your product and the level of support you provide. This is in spite of the few troubles that you have had along the way.

3. You believe that the customer will survey the market and meet with both your largest competitor and a smaller, more cost-effective organization.

4. Your management team is concerned about profitability. Full fee for a consulting project of this magnitude would be $100,000. Your management has asked you to both close the sale and NOT reduce your prices by more than 15 percent.

5. A quick look at your sales goals and the calendar tells you that this deal will go a long way towards helping you reach your quota for the quarter. You must have this sale and you must have it now!

So, you are being sent in to negotiate the close of a consulting project. If you take a look at the facts, you should be able to start to fill out your negotiating settlement range for the price variable.

For purposes of understanding the important and complex notion of how to synthesize a deal, we are going to keep this deal simple and focused on price even though it would constitute a direct violation of Paul and Peter's Rule of One: Never let the sales negotiation simplify to only one negotiating variable. If you do this, you put yourself in a situation where you must lose, no matter what.

So let's take a look at Figure 6-1 and start to complete our settlement range for the price negotiating variable.

	Seller	Buyer
FIGURE 6-1. CASE STUDY: SETTLEMENT RANGES DO NOT OVERLAP		
Maximum Supportable Position	100,000	Deal Breaker
Really Asking	90,000	Most Acceptable Agreement
Least Acceptable Position	85,000	Really Offering
Deal Breaker	84,999	Minimum Supportable Position

If you look at point 4 above, you can see that the seller's Maximum Supportable Position is $100,000. Why? Because this is essentially the list price of the consulting project. By saying "full fee" we mean that we are delivering on the consulting project without discounting on our price at all.

If you also look at point 4, you can see that the Least Acceptable Position is $85,000, because your management team has said that they will not accept a deal at a discount greater than 15 percent. So the $100,000 list price, less the 15 percent discount, gives us $85,000.

Using our definition for the Deal Breaker, you can see that the Deal Breaker is one unit of measure beneath the Least Acceptable Position. In our case, this would be $1 and the Deal Breaker would become $84,999.

The case study never really tells us the Really Asking position. We are supposed to determine that ourselves when we prepare for the negotiation. For purposes of our illustration, let us say that the Really Asking position for the seller is $90,000.

So, Figure 6-1 shows us the settlement range for price for the seller in our case study. Now, let's take a look at the buyer through their own eyes:

Buyer's Facts

1. Your company has been using XYZ Company's product for years. You have always felt that their product is technically superior to the competition. Further, you have always been happy with the support you receive and would like to continue your commitment to your existing supplier.

2. A new need has arisen within your business. You have called in your existing supplier, the company in our case study, to see if they can help.

3. You have already met with one of their very small competitors. You think the smaller competitor can do the work *but are not really sure*. They have bid $40,000 for the project. You have never worked with this (new, second) group before and you are concerned about the outcome of the project. After all, if the project is unsuccessful, you may lose your job.

4. You have also had a recent meeting with your supplier's major competitor. You do not believe that their product will perform as well as the one that you are using. In fact, industry data suggests that this larger competitor's product will diminish production in your factory by 2 percent when compared to your existing supplier. You anticipate manufacturing about $5,000,000 of this new product in its first full year of production. The $5,000,000 is your selling price. (Note: We are not going to discuss this in this book but the $5,000,000 in sales of the new product and the 2 percent manufacturing difference would be necessary for the seller to show the buyer why they are a better alternative in spite of the $50,000 worth of free product discussed in point 5.)

5. Your supplier's major competitor has bid $100,000 for the consulting project and has agreed to include $50,000 worth of free product with their proposal. The net cost of their proposal is therefore, $50,000.

6. Today, you are meeting with XYZ Company, your existing supplier. Your goal is to negotiate a deal. However, you cannot ignore competitive factors. Since you are using the XYZ Company product now, you expect that they will be pricey on their consulting proposal.

7. You have an existing budget in place for $60,000. You need to get rolling on this project immediately as your boss is going to look closely at the production yield on this project.

8. If you need to, you can take an additional $10,000 for this project from the budget of another project. A project expenditure above this amount may have a strong, negative impact on your career.

So, these are the facts of the case from the buyer's perspective. Now, let's take a look at their settlement range for price. This is portrayed in Figure 6-2 along with the information that we have already completed for the seller.

Please note that the following discussion assumes that we are looking at the case study facts through the eyes of the buyer. As a seller, you would likely not have access to this sort of information.

From point 3 above (in the buyer's portion of the case study), you can probably surmise that the buyer's Minimum Supportable Position is $40,000, because he cannot risk not having a vendor for the consulting project and $40,000 is the lowest offer the buyer received.

The buyer's Most Acceptable Position is probably $70,000. This is equal to the $60,000 that they have budgeted for the project (point 7) plus the $10,000 they can get from another project as described in point 8. So their Most Acceptable Position is $70,000 and their Deal Breaker is $70,001. Although we do not know what their Really Offering position is, for illustration purposes, we are going to say it is $50,000. The Really Offering and the Really Asking positions are something that would be determined by the buyer and the seller either individually or in conjunction with others in their organization during the planning phase of the negotiation.

FIGURE 6-2. CASE STUDY: SETTLEMENT RANGES DO NOT OVERLAP ADDING BUYER'S PERSPECTIVE

	Seller	*Buyer*	
Maximum Supportable Position	100,000	70,001	Deal Breaker
Really Asking	90,000	70,000	Most Acceptable Agreement
Least Acceptable Position	85,000	50,000	Really Offering
Deal Breaker	84,999	40,000	Minimum Supportable Position

Figure 6-3 clearly shows us the challenge at hand. As you can see, our Least Acceptable Position is $85,000. The customer's Maximum Acceptable Agreement is only $70,000.

Your management would rather not have the deal, than close the deal at less than $85,000. So, this is clearly and firmly as low as you can go.

On the customer's side, they are out of money. They cannot spend more than $70,000.

In a situation such as this, we are in a very difficult position. Why? Because there is no flexibility left from either side and the buyer has alternatives that will likely work for them. They have the smaller competitor who has proposed $40,000 and they have the larger competitor who has proposed essentially $50,000 ($100,000 for the consulting project, less $50,000 in free products).

In this case, the seller would ask the buyer if they could go any higher. After all, the buyer does really like us. The buyer, on the other hand would ask the seller if they could go any lower. Since both answers are no, it would seem like we have to walk away from the deal, even though we were the preferred provider and the business will go to one of our two competitors.

Ouch!

But it doesn't have to be like this. It doesn't have to be like this if you know how to synthesize a deal. The reason this is such an important skill for us is that the buyer will always have an alternative that will meet their needs. So, if we cannot create a deal for them where one does not exist (i.e., synthesize the deal), we will lose a lot of business.

FIGURE 6-3. CASE STUDY: SETTLEMENT RANGES DO NOT OVERLAP
WHY YOU NEED TO SYNTHESIZE A DEAL

	Seller	*Buyer*	
Maximum Supportable Position	100,000	70,001	Deal Breaker
Really Asking	90,000	70,000	Most Acceptable Agreement
Least Acceptable Position	85,000	50,000	Really Offering
Deal Breaker	84,999	40,000	Minimum Supportable Position

Ways to Synthesize a Deal

There are a great many approaches you should explore in your attempt to synthesize a deal. We look at them in this chapter, one by one and in some detail, to see how we might apply them to the situation we are looking at in our case study.

Deferred Payment

Defer a portion of the payment to a new budget cycle. This is relatively easy to implement and is an often overlooked tool of the sales professional. Using our case study to illustrate how this would work, there is a $15,000 gap between the price that we need and the most that the customer can pay. The customer's budget gap could be an artificial budget gap.

What this means is that the customer has a limit on their funds for this quarter or this year. However, next quarter or next year, there may be additional budget dollars available.

In this case, you could ask the customer if it would be helpful if you could defer a portion of the price or payment until the next accounting cycle. This accounting cycle can either be the next quarter or the next year. Actually, it may even be the next month. So you propose an alternative to the customer (synthesizing the deal) that they pay $70,000 now and defer the remaining $15,000 to the next accounting cycle.

You could even take your deal one step further. Since you will be deferring a portion of your payment to the next accounting cycle, you may want to consider accelerating the portion of the payment that you are receiving now.

Expanding on our example, let us assume that you have to defer the remaining $15,000 payment until the next quarter. This could be two months or more away. Since you will be deferring a portion of your payment to accommodate the customer, you may ask for something of equal or greater value in return.

Let's say that the normal payment terms for a consulting project are a 50 percent deposit to secure the project and a 50 percent payment upon project completion. Under these circumstances, you could ask your customer to provide you a 90 percent deposit upon contract signing and the remaining 10 percent upon project completion.

The reason that we did not ask for a 100 percent deposit is because the customer would explain that under the 100 percent scenario they would have no insurance that the project would be completed in a timely and complete manner.

In fact, the customer may not like this idea at all because of the reason noted. They would have no insurance that we would complete the project in a timely and satisfactory manner. However, because we invest in negotiation planning, we are prepared. That is why we have the next synthesis point.

Adding Interest on Deferred Payment

Consider adding interest to compensate for the deferred payment. This is a point that is very important to us as sales professionals in the context of creating a win/win outcome. After all, if it were us lending the customer the $15,000, I'm sure we would want to be compensated for the use of our funds.

To implement this idea in the classic sense where we actually perform an interest calculation would probably unnecessarily complicate the procurement process and may even defer the closing of the sale, which is not at all what we are looking to do. An open deal is always at risk so we want to take the customer out of the market as soon as we can by completing the sales negotiation process.

If we were to do an interest calculation, it may look as follows. Let us assume that the current interest rate is 7 percent, we are deferring $15,000 of our purchase price to the next account period, and that there are two months to go until the customer can actually make the payment. These two months are also assumed to be in excess of normal trade terms for a project of this type.

So, the interest calculation might look as follows. First, we would take the $15,000 and multiply it by our assumed interest rate of 7 percent. This would yield an interest charge of $1,050 if we were to defer the payment of $15,000 for an entire year.

However, we know that we are not deferring the payment for an entire year. Rather, we are only deferring payment for two months so the next part of the calculation would be to take the interest charge of $1,050 and adjust it for the two months out of the entire year that we are extending the payment for. In order to do this we would multiply the $1,050 by 2/12ths. This would result in a final interest charge of $175. This is the opportunity cost of allowing the customer to defer the payment of the $15,000 for two months.

So, we could charge the customer $15,175 for their final payment or we could charge them some other amount to mask the fact that we are actually adding interest to account for the payment deferral. For example, if we were to charge the customer $15,250 or $15,500, we could avoid the discussion of whether we are adding actual interest into the calculation.

These other amounts (the $250 or $500) also account for the cost of additional processing due to the payment deferral which is not part of your standard operating procedure. So, returning to the total contract value, you could simply say that $85,000 is the pay-now price and $85,500 is the deferred-payment price. These amounts include the non-deferred portion of the contract amount ($70,000), the budget gap of $15,000 and the pseudo interest charge of $500.

Differential Pricing for the Life of Contract

Consider offering a lower price in year one and a higher price in years two and three. This option may work for you if you are in the type of business where you can negotiate multiyear or long-term supply contracts.

So, in our case study, the customer had a "real" budget of $60,000 and an additional budget of $10,000 that they could take advantage of if absolutely necessary.

We also know that the customer uses outside consultants quite frequently and that they will have a need for your types of services in years two and three. What they do not know is the type of need that they will have and what decision a lengthy vendor evaluation process would have produced.

So, what we could do is agree to take the existing project for $60,000. This would give the customer two major advantages. First, they would not have to reach into that other budget that we have been referring to. Second, they would not have to go through a lengthy and costly vendor evaluation process in years two and three. (Our work has indicated that a typical vendor selection process at a relatively large organization could cost the customer up to $50,000 each time they have to go through the process of vendor selection.)

So, we agree to take this project for $60,000 and the customer agrees to provide us with two subsequent projects similar to the one we are discussing now in years two and three (though it can be sooner if need arises sooner). Once a fee is agreed upon between the customer and us for these latter projects, we add an additional $20,000 to the first subsequent project and an additional $20,000 to the second subsequent project.

Ignoring the time value of money, which would only unnecessarily add to the complexity of the calculation, the customer is getting the first project for $60,000 (which is what they wanted) and we are effectively getting the first project for $100,000 (which is what our management had wanted).

Also, in case you are concerned about the second and third projects, remember that we have yet to spec out those projects or negotiate their related project fees. The second project, when it arises could be a project worth $50,000, $100,000 or even larger. Whatever the project fees are for the second and third projects, we will add an additional $20,000 to the cost of each project to make up for the fact that it wasn't included in the current project amount.

This is a great example of how to synthesize a deal.

Share Customer's Future Profits

Accept a lower price in year one and consider ways to share in the rewards in years two and three. This idea is simply a riskier version of the option we just discussed. Here, we take the $60,000 price in year one, and we share in the customer's success in years two and three. For simplicity's sake, we could take additional payments to the extent of 5 percent of the impact of our work.

So, if we were going to help them launch a new product, we could calculate our additional payments each year (or each quarter) equal to the sales of their new product times their gross profit percentage (to account for their cost of goods sold) times 5 percent (our incremental fee entitlement).

The good thing about this method of synthesizing the deal is that there is no real upper boundary to the payments we receive. Depending on the success of the customer, we could get additional payments of $100,000, $200,000 or even more. Who knows—and that is exactly the point. Using this method, there is really no upper boundary to our success. We could ultimately get paid double and even triple the price we were asking in the original negotiation.

The bad thing about this method of synthesizing the deal is that we could get nothing additional in the form of payments for a number of reasons. First, the customer could be unsuccessful with the new item they are making; second, it could take them more than two years to really start to sell it, and third, their costs in the early years of production might be quite a bit higher until they really become adept at making this new item.

However, as we mentioned in the beginning of this discussion, this is a long-standing customer. It is one that you probably know quite a bit about so if you are going to make this type of arrangement (which is actually fairly common in many technology industries where one company's product gets imbedded into another company's product), this might be the time to try it. Clearly, you will want to have a reasonable expectation of at least getting your $100,000 if not a decent amount more because you are bearing the risk of only getting $60,000 when your company can ill afford such a discount. This type of transaction would have to be discussed with your management *prior to* broaching the topic with the customer.

Be Creative!

Consider other trade-offs. Take a look at all the variables that we have listed as impacting a sales negotiation. Incorporate them into your deal in any way that makes sense to you and your management. Hopefully, it will make sense to your customer as well. There are no limits to possibility when you synthesize a deal.

Conclusion

Synthesizing a deal is one of the most crucial skills that you can learn. Yes, there is a little art and creativity to the process, but underlying every critical element in sales is a *process* that you can learn and improve upon.

The need to synthesize a deal comes about when the settlement ranges of the seller and the buyer do not overlap. In that situation, you will not be able to make up the difference by meeting the customer halfway. Rather, you will really need to understand the customer's business, needs, interests, and positions, everything that we have discussed so far, to create a win/win outcome where no outcome seemed possible prior to your deal synthesis.

*   *   *

Part Two of this book focuses on strategies and tactics in professional sales negotiations. Before we focus on tactics, we begin, in Chapter 7, with an overview of the personality types you will be dealing with in your negotiations. We show you how to use this understanding of personality to best deal with whoever sits across the negotiating table from you.

Part Two

Negotiating
Tactics

CHAPTER 7

Using Negotiating Styles to Gain Advantage

Wouldn't it be great if you had psychic powers that enabled you to read your customers' minds? You could just take one look at them and know exactly the right words to say—and not to say—in order to achieve that much-needed win/win. You'd be the world's most successful negotiator, right?

Well, we can't help you develop psychic powers, but we can help you learn how to profile your customers using a simple technique that will give you the advantage in your business deals.

Why do you need to profile your customers? Because in sales negotiations it's easy to focus too much on the end result—closing the deal—and forget about the fact that you're dealing with human beings complete with their own emotions, value systems, with differing backgrounds and viewpoints. Human beings are unpredictable, so learning how to analyze your customer quickly can take some of the uncertainty out of the equation.

There are a number of popular systems for categorizing people's behavior or personality styles. Using any of these techniques can help make working relationships smoother and more effective.

For sales negotiations, we favor a technique derived from the book, *Personal Styles and Effective Performance: Make Your Style Work for You*, by D. W. Merrill and R. H. Reid (London: CRC Press, 1999) because it is easy to apply in the field as you enter the sales negotiation process. Learning how to make certain observations about your customers will allow you to categorize them into one of four behavioral styles: Analytical, Driver, Amiable, and Expressive. Knowing your customer's personality style will help you predict how they'll behave in a negotiation and help you determine how you should behave to orchestrate the all-important win/win.

Perhaps you should analyze your own personality style before going on to study your customers. Start by asking yourself this question: In your business dealings and interactions, do you make your decisions based more on a fact basis or on a feeling basis? For example, if you are more formal, cool, guarded, cautious, and harder to get to know, for the purposes of this self-analysis, we'll call you a "fact" person. If in your business dealings you're more open, informal, permissive, a good communicator and easy to get to know, we'll say you're a "feeling" person. (Don't worry if you're not 100 percent one way or the other, just think about which of the two categories you tend to lean toward.)

Next, think about whether you'd describe yourself as a little more talkative or a little more reserved. If you have strong opinions, make a lot of statements, and are very competitive in business, we'll call you a "tell" person. If you're a little more reserved, thoughtful, and cooperative and you ask lots of questions, we'll say you're an "ask" person.

The Four Behavioral Styles

The four distinct behavioral types mentioned above emerge when you combine the traits of "fact" or "feeling" with "ask" or "tell," as you can see from the style grid presented in Figure 7-1. An Ask/Fact person is called an "Analytical," a Fact/Tell person is called a "Driver," a "Tell/Feel" person is an "Expressive," and an "Ask/Feel" person is an "Amiable."

FIGURE 7-1. BEHAVIORAL STYLE GRID

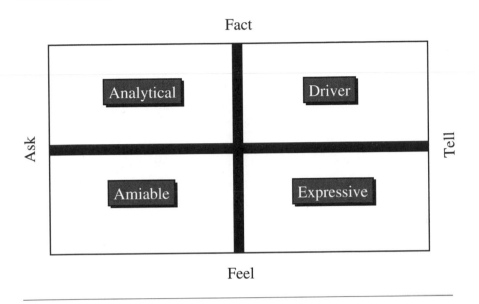

Before we go any further, it's important to remember that we're not making moral judgments here. There's no good or bad, just different. You may be interested to know that a number of recent past U.S. presidents came from each of these four categories so it doesn't matter which one you profile out into. Each of those presidents was successful in his career, which shows that success can come from anywhere. What we're saying is, just because you're one style or another, it doesn't mean you're going to be a better negotiator or a worse negotiator, a better salesperson or a worse salesperson—or a better president or a worse president.

All you need to remember is that you will naturally negotiate according to the traits of predominantly one of these four styles—and so will your customer. If your styles aren't compatible, your negotiation may not be as successful as it otherwise could be. However, as the salesperson or the account manager, you can learn how to analyze your buyer and how to customize your natural negotiating style to the type of behavior your customer will relate to.

You cannot totally change who you are just to please the buyer and close the deal—nor should you try to change your personality style.

Analytical

Analytical negotiators are polite but reserved. They like to gather lots of information and be presented with a mountain of facts; they tend to be a little more serious and take very detailed notes.

In their decision-making, Analyticals like to have time to digest all the information you give them. They like all their questions answered in great detail because they are so diligent and process-oriented. They don't do business based on gut feelings or hunches; they make their decisions based on cold, hard facts.

Analyticals don't beat around the bush or waste time in idle chit-chat. They simply like to get down to business. You'll have a good idea as to whether your customer is an Analytical the minute you walk into their office. It will be very neat and tidy, with no superfluous decorations like flowers and plants. Papers will be stacked neatly in their trays and you might see some framed awards, charts, and graphs on the walls. Above all, what you'll notice most is how immaculate this person's office is.

Driver

These high achievers are very results-oriented and not afraid of taking risks or bullying to get those results. Drivers usually only look for summary information rather than piles of detail, so save that for the Analytical buyers. Drivers just want you to give them the bottom line and can get pretty impatient and frustrated if you waste time getting there. But don't worry, you won't be playing any guessing games, they'll come right out and tell you if you're taking too long giving them what they want.

Drivers are *demanding*, with a capital *D*. They are very thorough, and like the Analyticals, they base their decisions on facts. They are extroverted, forceful, and decisive. If you come out of a negotiation feeling exhausted by a buyer's overbearing nature, you can bet you've just been bowled over by a Driver.

Drivers' persuasiveness and decisiveness can easily catch you off guard in a negotiation if you're not adequately prepared, so be warned. Like the Analytical buyer, a Driver's office will be a picture of perfect organization. But while the Analytical's office is more utilitarian and sparse, a Driver's office is decked out for maximum impact, with the most expensive furniture, spectacular views and exotic plants—the typical power office.

Amiable

This friendly, fuzzy, feeling-oriented negotiator is much more easygoing and cooperative than the Analyticals or the Drivers. They're very responsive to others, interested in other people's opinions, and will want to know about the relationships that are formed in a negotiation more than the nitty-gritty facts and figures. The Amiable is the quintessential team player.

Amiables are dependable and often a pleasure to negotiate with—until you ask them to take a risk or make a decision that is! They prefer more stable working environments and will shy away from making a decision unless everyone in the organization from the CEO to the janitor has agreed.

Amiables, by their very nature, work towards creating harmonious relationships and they never forget a slight, so keep everything nice and aboveboard. They'll appreciate you asking about their family, their interests, their hobbies. They don't see this as a waste of time, like a Driver would, but as an important part of building rapport.

Amiables will plug away at a deal, working conscientiously and consistently until they've negotiated what they feel is fair for all concerned. When negotiating with an Amiable buyer, you'll need to explain how the deal is going to benefit them, their coworkers, the coworkers' cats . . . No, not really, but you get the idea. They like to confer with others, so make lots and lots of copies of your proposals. The Amiables' need to run everything by their coworkers and superiors can make them painstakingly slow negotiators but hey, if you do the right thing by them you'll have a friend for life!

You can easily distinguish an Amiable's office from say, an Analytical's or a Driver's office, as it will be much more homey, with pictures of family and friends decorating the desk and some well-tended plants and colorful pictures or paintings on the walls.

Expressive

Just like our friends the Amiables, Expressives are very feeling-oriented and they make great efforts to ensure their business relationships are healthy and that everyone feels part of the team. You'll feel they're bending over backwards to support you and make you feel included and important, so much so that you may never get a word in edgeways. Their enthusiasm, diplomacy, and ability to inspire others easily win people over, and their engaging personality is what will first strike you about Expressive negotiators.

The difference between Expressives and Amiables is that Expressives are a lot more assertive and a lot more talkative. They're also fairly disorganized. Their office might look like a disaster zone, but don't make the mistake of judging them by the messy office. Somewhere among those piles of papers and notes stuck all over the desk is exactly the piece of information they need—and they can find it in a jiffy.

These flamboyant characters might seem all over the place, like they couldn't close a deal if you paid them, but they're often among the best salespeople and negotiators due to their sheer exuberance and charisma. Expressives hate paperwork and like to make decisions based on gut feelings. They'll be happy to chat about your proposal over a coffee and will do most of the talking, but you'll lose them pretty quickly if you present them with a bunch of reports they need to wade through. How boring!

Above all, Expressives love all things new and innovative, so highlight these aspects of your proposal and you'll definitely spark their interest.

Exercise

Think of one of your largest clients. Are they a Fact or Feeling person? An Ask or Tell person? (Refer to Figure 7-1.) Ask yourself these three questions:

1. How would you tailor your approach so that it was compatible to their style? What types of questions would you ask?

2. How would you present your information?

3. How would you customize your own personality to appeal to them? What words do you think would appeal to them?

Customizing Your Approach

The exercise above is designed to encourage you to start thinking about how you can tailor your negotiating style to suit different clients. As I mentioned earlier, its your job as the salesperson to customize your approach to suit the behavioral style of your customer, so let's go through each behavioral style and analyze how best to do that.

Negotiating with an Analytical

The key words to remember when negotiating with an Analytical is the old Boy Scout motto: Be Prepared.

Let's say you're an Expressive. Your natural tendency is to be a bit of a joker but if you went into a negotiation with a results-oriented Analytical making wisecracks, it probably wouldn't go down too well, as Analyticals like to get down to business and focus on the task at hand. What will impress them is if you have detailed facts on every part of your proposal ready, because you can bet your life an Analytical is going to want those before he or she makes any decisions. You will need to be very precise with every part of your presentation or you can kiss your deal good-bye.

An Analytical likes to go away and digest all the information in your proposal, so don't go into the negotiation with guns blazing, ready to close the deal right then and there, which is probably what a Driver would do. Use the first meeting as a chance to present a detailed proposal where you stick with the facts and answer any questions the Analytical might have. Then, make a time for a follow-up meeting where you'll hopefully be able to complete the negotiation. Analyticals respond well to deadlines, so make it clear that you'll be expecting to close the deal in the second or third meeting.

Consider sending the information ahead of time so that when you actually meet your customer, they'll have had a chance to analyze your data. This might even save you a follow-up trip.

When you're working with an Analytical they'll want to go through the numbers thoroughly and they'll want a lot of justification for the positions you're taking in the negotiation. They'll ask you, "How did you calculate those figures?" Or, "How much of a discount will you give me if I buy five hundred units?" Then, after they ponder your answers for a while, they may ask you the same questions again just to be doubly sure they've got a handle on everything, so be prepared to repeat yourself.

For example, let's say you wanted to charge an Analytical client a management fee of $500,000. You can bet your bottom dollar they're going to want to know what they're getting for that money in intricate detail, so itemize each of the services so they know exactly what each one is offering and what its market value is. You won't get very far with an Analytical if you say, "For $500,000 we'll give you a little bit of this and a little bit of that; we'll mix it all up and what comes out we'll call a management fee." That would fly with an Expressive or an Amiable, but not an Analytical or a Driver.

If you're more on the feeling side (Expressive or Amiable) it won't be your natural tendency to be so fact-based in your approach, so you'll need to extend yourself to play ball the way your Analytical client likes it to be played.

It's also crucial to change your vocabulary to suit an Analytical person. Instead of asking, "How do you *feel* about this?" ask "What do you *think* about this?" Analyticals don't feel anything about anything when it comes to business, so stay strictly in the realm of hard facts and logical thoughts, focusing on words like "think" and "goal," not soft words like "feel" and "vision." Uses phrases like, "Boy, if we could get this done it would support your goals" rather than, "If we could get this done it would support your vision."

Remember, always go into a negotiation with an Analytical fully prepared to justify your position and answer any questions they fire at you. Lead the negotiation with confidence.

I'm predominantly Analytical in my business negotiations and I had a very successful negotiation with a fellow Analytical who was second in charge of a large Australian retailer. Let's call him Bill. I was approached by this organization, as were a number of other firms, to take on a large brief within the group. Being an Analytical, Bill not only wanted a measurable outcome and return on investment, he wanted a partner in his business to share a bit of the pain. What he really wanted was to have a relationship with an individual or organization and gain a sense of knowing they were there with him through the journey.

It was a long negotiation, but I sensed through my questioning that the reason he ultimately chose our firm was that we offered him the feeling of security he was looking for. He was asking, "Do I feel that this person is the person I can work side-by-side with for a number of years?" When he and I got on the same page, the negotiation of price became a secondary issue. What mattered was the relationship. This was a case of two Analyticals who simply clicked.

But it's not always that easy to negotiate with an Analytical, especially for say, an action-oriented Driver. Ken is a Driver colleague of mine who found negotiating with an Analytical utterly frustrating. He was selling a technical product and the buyer, who was an engineer, wanted infinite detail of the product. Throughout the negotiation, Ken was trying to move forward and close the deal in typical Driver fashion, while the Analytical engineer wanted to keep focusing on the details. The more Ken pushed to get things closed off, the more the engineer pulled back. They simply couldn't have a meeting of the minds because they just couldn't communicate. According to Ken, as a Driver he just couldn't handle being asked for that amount of detail. The buyer ended up awarding the deal to a fellow engineer who was able to give him the detail he required.

This case study brings up an interesting point. Ken was well aware of the four personality styles before going into this negotiation. He knew this guy was a hardcore Analytical. Despite that awareness, he couldn't override his own natural style to drive forward. Sometimes, when you're a square peg trying to fit a round hole, you might start to think, "I'm really just not going to make this happen." And sometimes when you do have such an intense personality clash with your buyer all you can do is simply walk away or suggest they transfer to another colleague.

However, if you're not one for giving in, your goal needs to become staying focused on trying to mold yourself. If you have an intense Driver trying to talk to a 100 percent Analytical, the Driver will always be thinking, "C'mon, how much more do you need?" You can mask those feelings, but you can't always hide them over the course of a long negotiation.

So, what we can learn from this story is that if you can take off your Driver's hat and put on your Analytical's hat (or whichever style is appropriate to your negotiation), for not just ten minutes but for an hour and a half, then there is a far greater likelihood that you will be able to close the business.

Negotiating with a Driver

One thing you can count on when negotiating with a Driver is that your meetings are going to be quick! Drivers like to get down to business and they don't like to mess around with superfluous information or casual conversation. With this in mind, you don't want to get pushed around in your meeting by an impatient Driver or be intimidated by their demands for on-the-spot decisions.

Again, it's important to go into the negotiation well-prepared. While you still need to have all the background information ready to support your position, you'll do better with a Driver if you present a concise summary of the benefits, features, and advantages of your proposal and base your arguments on facts, not feelings. Use bullet points and have supporting data available to back up each point if needed. Your language should be strong and concise and your conversation should focus on expected results. Drivers can't stand wasting time, so the faster and more to the point you can be in your presentation, the better.

A seller going into a negotiation with a Driver needs to be very confident and focused on getting to the end result pretty quickly. The danger here is you could be pushed into making a decision you're not comfortable with by a Driver if you allow yourself to be pressured. This is more likely to happen to an Amiable or an Expressive than a fellow Driver or an Analytical. You'll need to be ready to fight for the integrity of your position and have a few clever delaying tactics up your sleeve.

Something I do a little differently when negotiating with a Driver is have a few open-ended questions ready. These are questions that require detailed answers, rather than just one-word answers like yes or no. The way to manage a Driver and control the direction of the conversation is to make sure you're the one asking the questions. The person who asks the questions is the person who controls the direction of the conversation. You can't get in their way and start challenging them and out-talking them, but what you can do is deflect their direction by asking them lots of open-ended questions (more about these in Chapter 8) and really get at the interests of the negotiation, not the positions of the negotiation.

Calling on Higher Authority is another way to avoid being backed into a corner by a Driver (see Chapter 9 for more on Higher Authority). A Driver will say, "I'm a decision-maker and I'm going to make a decision about this right now." If you're not sure you're ready to make a decision or you don't like the direction the negotiation is taking, rather than make the wrong decision under pressure, simply say, "That's a great point and I think I can support you but I'm going to have to bounce it off my boss/the committee."

It's also important to have a few different options prepared, as you don't want to find yourself in a position where a Driver outright rejects your first proposal and you have nothing else to come back with. Have your options clearly mapped out and go in strong and convincing, and you'll avoid being spun into a frenzy by the dynamite Driver.

My Driver colleague Ken recently closed a deal with a stockbroker who was a high Driver, the kind of guy who thinks at a million miles an hour and needs a result almost immediately. I had met this client three months earlier and hadn't managed to close the deal. Here's the story in Ken's words:

"This guy I totally understood. It was one of those meetings you have where you're really conscious of the whole style of the other person. I sat back in the chair and he sat forward, fully cranked into it and I had to change to his style to keep up. He was a total extrovert. I had to push myself to my Driver limit to match this guy. It was a matter of, 'I feel your pain, this is what you need, this can heal your pain, we can do it next week.' We closed the deal the following Monday. I recognized that he was a highly driven person and adapted to fit his style without pondering the decision too long."

Ken didn't have to totally alter his personality to do the deal in this case, but he did have to up the ante somewhat. When I met that same client three months prior, had I known he was such a high Driver, I would have really altered my own Analytical style. I'm usually very matter-of-fact when I talk about my business, but in hindsight I could have closed the deal with that guy if I had left out the detail and just said, "Yep, let's lock it and load it."

Here's another story that illustrates how adapting to match the buyer's style can sometimes be crucial in a negotiation. The HR department of a large automobile distributorship had asked my firm to submit a bid for a sales training program. I submitted a quote to HR, then started discussions with two women in HR, and I felt that we were very much on the same page.

The two women gave me a heads-up on the general manager of the company, who was the final decision-maker. When I met him I suggested that we needed to do a lot of research throughout their dealerships to understand where their dealers were at and what they wanted in terms of training, rather than just tell them what training they were going to get.

I tried to explain the value of that to the general manager and this guy just shut me down. He was adamant that he would tell his dealer network what they needed, whereas in my sixteen years of business I'd learned that if we could get buy-in from everyone, they would feel they had participated in creating their training program and it would be a lot more successful.

The feedback I received from the HR manager and the training manager was that the general manager wasn't open to any suggestions whatsoever other than his own. From that experience I learned that I should have just listened, understood that he was a Driver and nonnegotiable. Had I delivered the credit, power, and influence to him, he would have agreed to my proposal.

I had an ethical problem with that situation because I did not believe his position was in the best interests of the shareholders, so in that case I was happy to walk away from the deal. I believed what he wanted was not the best practice and would not get the best result. Remember, the outcome is long remembered after the negotiation, so sometimes it's better to walk away.

However, if I had not been in business for myself and was working for a company and my primary motivator was money, I would have changed my approach, knowing what I know about how an Analytical should do business with a Driver. My proposal was inclusive of strategies that would value add to the selling solution and this Driver wasn't the slightest bit interested in any of that. He just wanted me to train his people in telephone techniques: presenting, negotiating, and closing. That is the archaic mindset of the old-school auto industry. If I had just agreed to do what he asked, I could have closed the deal. The magic words would have been, "If I come back to you with a proposal based around your budget parameters am I correct in assuming that we're going forward?"

So, after this experience, my advice to anyone dealing with a Driver who is determined to close the deal, ethics aside, is to listen attentively to the proposal, feed back your understanding of exactly what they want, get confirmation on that, and then progress quickly to price negotiation and closing strategies.

Negotiating with an Amiable

Amiables are more feeling-oriented so they'll respond to you better if you lead with a soft approach and follow up with the facts later. Don't be too heavy-handed or go in for the hard sell. Just be relaxed and agreeable. Give them copies of your sales information because they'll want to hand it out to their colleagues and seek their opinions before making any decisions.

Due to the Amiable's inherent nature to want to confer with others, they'll often use Higher Authority on you, a situation you should try and avoid. Paul and I always say it's really hard to negotiate with a ghost. If you want to negotiate, you have to have all the parties at the table, but Amiables are renowned for wanting to refer back to a committee or whoever is going to give them the approval they seek. So, here's a perfect opportunity for you to use their own negotiating style on them and to try and get that committee in the room with you. You need to be able to negotiate with the true decision-makers, so take advantage of the Amiable's desire to have everybody's support by encouraging them to bring the committee to your meeting.

In any negotiation it's important that you never assume that the person you are dealing with is the final decision-maker. Always ask! I can give you plenty of examples where a buyer will talk as if they have the authority to make the final decision and just when you're about to close the deal, they'll tell you they have to confer with a boss or a colleague or a committee, especially if they're an Amiable. If they come back with a no, you've wasted a lot of time.

I was negotiating with Bruce, the general manager of a large construction company in Western Australia. Bruce approached me to conduct some work for him and he was an Amiable through and through. He emphatically said yes to everything in my proposal. He continually said, "That's great, I'm really comfortable with that, that's exactly what I want." But I found that, to protect his own position, he had brought the proposal to the managing director. Bruce's amiable and positive manner was a little deceiving, and I hadn't confirmed whether there was anyone else involved in the final decision. Big mistake. Fortunately, in this case, he came back with a yes and the deal went through, but I could have easily been caught out on that one. The golden rule when dealing with an Amiable—indeed, any of the four personality styles—is to ask: "Is there anyone else in addition to yourself involved in the final decision?"

Another trait of Amiables is that they tend to ask "why?" a lot, so be prepared to answer their questions and use the word "we" to appeal to their sense of being a team player, and present your proposal in a friendly, unhurried manner. If you're also an Amiable, that will be a piece of cake, but if you're a talkative Driver or Expressive, avoid that inherent trait of yours to talk up a storm. Amiables like people who listen, but they won't ask you to stop blabbering and listen, they'll just clam up and before you know it, you've lost the deal. Drivers will especially need to wear their sensitivity caps here, to avoid railroading the Amiable.

Negotiating with an Expressive

This is one personality type you may end up fighting with for control of the negotiations. They work off their gut instincts, and they're also very talkative so they find it easy to direct the negotiation. You'll need a good list of questions up your sleeve to avoid getting pushed around. You'll also find it useful to invoke Higher Authority if they pressure you to make a decision before you're ready.

When communicating with an Expressive, ask them how they feel about different aspects of your proposal, rather than what they think, and try to mirror their enthusiasm. Go into the negotiation with a friendly demeanor, engage them in a bit of chitchat, perhaps comment on something you like in their office or on what they're wearing. Expressives are very image-conscious and you're more likely to succeed if you can explain how your product or service is going to enhance their image.

I'd like to illustrate how appealing to the ego of the image-conscious Expressive can work. I was once negotiating with a typical Expressive whom I'll call David. He was very outgoing and verbose and led me to believe that he was a great leader of his people. The truth of the matter was that he wasn't a leader, he didn't know what his people wanted, and his people didn't respect him. He was actually *oblivious* to their needs. I had to negotiate away from what he wanted—but he still wanted ownership of the solution. So I shifted it from making it all about him to making it about the share price, which was ultimately going to reflect on him. I appealed to his ego by saying, "You can still own this new solution." When I presented the program to the Board, I said, "With your permission, David, I would like to share with the entire organization the input you've had in this solution. You've been absolutely fantastic and given me great guidance and I think that's a credit to you." Today, that client is a massive account of mine, and it all started with that tricky negotiation.

Tailoring your presentation to appeal to an Expressive can be very important, as you'll lose them if you present them with a bunch of boring reports. They prefer more visual material, like charts and colorful pictures, and you should only pull the more detailed factual information out of your briefcase when asked for it. Expressives like summaries up-front, so don't overwhelm them with too much detailed information at first. Expressives are storytellers, so allow them time to tell you their tales and anecdotes, and perhaps jump in with a couple of your own. They'll feel you're on the same page and really get what you're about, especially if you focus on being very open and responsive to whatever they are talking about.

Analytics often have trouble negotiating with Expressives. Primarily focused on the facts and figures, the Analytic wants to relay this information in a concise and efficient manner. However, the highly excitable Expressive doesn't care about the facts and figures and just wants to share all the amazing information they have bubbling around in their brain. If neither appreciates how the other is wired, the Expressive will tend to dominate the conversation and tell stories, leaving the

Analytical walking away from the negotiation thinking it was a complete waste of time.

Amiables may also find it tricky to negotiate with an Expressives, as they're naturally more prone to sit back and listen, so the negotiation can end up being very one-sided. If you're an Amiable trying to negotiate with an Expressive, bring along a list of questions you can pull out at opportune moments in order to lead the conversation in a direction you're comfortable with. One area where the Amiables will be compatible with the Expressives is that they both like to feel they have harmonious work relationships, so they'll both be working to avoid conflict and nurture the business relationship.

How to Analyze Your Customer Quickly

Using our quick analysis (see Figure 7-1), you'll be able to mold your approach for the best outcome.

Of course, this technique is easier to do in person. Although there is a little of all four behavioral styles in each of us, most of us tend to display more traits from one category than any other. This is our primary behavioral style. We also have a secondary style, which if you refer to the style grid in Figure 7-1, is usually one of the two styles that borders your primary style.

Whether you take this information on board and use it in your negotiating or not, the main point here is that as sales professionals our role is to go into the negotiation process in neutral, to be attentive, and to observe and mirror. The first ten seconds after you walk into the negotiating room are crucial. If the customer immediately pegs your personality style opposed to his or hers, the rest is gone. If you're struggling to work out which of the four personality types your buyer fits into, don't get hung up on it. Just tone your own traits down and mirror his or hers.

As I mentioned earlier, I don't subscribe to the philosophy that people can alter their personality to a huge degree. The idea is just to be aware that there are four personality types and you're not going to be a perfect fit for everyone. You have to leave your ego at the front door.

If you lose a deal it's easy to blame the prospect. "They're idiots, they only buy on price, they don't care about my service." It's easy to find reasons why you're not successful. However, you can value add by saying, "Maybe it was me and one of the reasons I was not successful is that I did not align myself to them." Part of that alignment process involves understanding their personality style and how to match it. The next time you fail to close a deal, say to yourself, "I actually just wasn't on the same page. What I can learn from this is that next time, I must more successfully realize that I'm not going to close this deal at all."

Summary

In a nutshell, this is what you need to understand:

- *Analyticals* need facts, figures, and data. Give an orderly presentation supported with documentation and allow them to examine the proposal in detail.

- *Amiables* need to know the human dimensions of the situation. Be friendly; they fell about that. Also, establish who the final decision-maker is on their end.

- *Expressives* are image-conscious and like to know why your product or service is the most exciting and innovative.

- *Drivers* require action and a solid strategy for implementing the deal. Tell them what you will do for them and how soon.

CHAPTER 8

Power Questioning Strategies

Successful negotiators ask a lot of questions. They ask the right questions at the right time, they listen to the answers, they acknowledge the other party's viewpoint, and they use follow-up questions to gain greater insight into the other party's interests.

Knowing the difference between the right and wrong questions to ask can mean the difference between success and failure. Even if you're not a skilled interviewer, you can still negotiate successfully with the world's largest company and hold your own in the toughest negotiation if you know how to use the right power questioning strategies. Conversely, you can lose deal after deal if you ask the wrong questions.

The two basic types of questions used in negotiating are open-ended questions and close-ended questions. Open-ended questions require a detailed response on the part of the participant whereas close-ended questions require a limited response, such as yes or no. "Do you like this blue sweater?" or "Would you like delivery this week or next?" are close-ended questions. An example of a good open-ended question is, "What are your goals and objectives?"

Open-ended questions are much better asked in the early stages of the negotiation and close-ended questions are better asked in the later stages of the negotiation. Why? Because open-ended questions are less intimidating and will allow you to learn more about your client so as to gain an overview of what they need from you. If you ask too many direct, close-ended questions in the beginning, you could scare them off, as you may come across as too aggressive. Also, by asking open-ended questions you allow them to share their interests with you without having to divulge their whole negotiating strategy.

Open-ended questions are not necessarily better than close-ended questions, they're just different tools to be used at different stages of the negotiation. In a toolbox you have a hammer and a screwdriver. They're both good tools, but one serves one function and the other serves another function. Likewise, in sales and negotiations you have open-ended and close-ended questions that serve different functions.

Do you want to know what one of the biggest problems with salespeople is when it comes to asking questions? When we're under pressure we ask too many close-ended questions. "Can't we close the deal now?" No. "Are you happy with my proposal?" No. "Is that your best price?" Yes. You get the idea.

In the early stages of the negotiation you need to be gathering information, figuring out what the other party's interests are, and making sure you've evaluated all of your options in terms of what the negotiation is all about. You're not even going to scratch the surface if all you do is ask questions that require a yes or no answer.

Most open-ended questions begin with one of the following words: How? What? When? Where? Why? Ask a question beginning with any of these words and you're asking for a detailed response. Here's a list of good open-ended questions:

- Could you give me an example?
- I'm not sure I follow your reasoning, could you explain that to me again?
- Could you describe that process?
- What would you suggest?
- How would you do it if you were in my shoes?

- How do you think we should proceed?

- Could you help me understand how you arrived at that conclusion?

- What if we were to come up with a payment plan to fit your budget?

- Please explain why you feel our product is not what you're looking for.

- What changes can we make here to achieve an outcome that is fair for both of us?

- What's your thinking behind that?

- Do you have any other ideas on how I could best meet your needs?

- I'd like to ask your advice on this.

- I'd be interested to know your opinion on that.

- What in addition to price is going to influence your final decision?

According to William Ury in his book, *Getting Past No*, one of the most powerful questions in the English language is "what if?" (Bantam, 1991, p. 65). Using "what if" in a negotiation encourages the other party to discuss options and allows you to introduce possible solutions without challenging their positions. Examples are:

- What if we were to stretch out the project so that the excess could go into next year's budget?

- What if we were to reduce the magnitude of the project to fit within your budget constraints?

- What if we can help you show your boss how the benefits to your company justify asking for a budget increase?

Your arsenal of open-ended questions are your tools of trade and you'll need to develop a good set that you can take with you into any negotiation, though they should be adapted to suit the person and type of company you're negotiating with.

These questions should also be prioritized in order of importance and have a logical flow to them. You need to have a negotiating strategy behind each one of your questions. To work this out, ask yourself, "What am I trying to accomplish here?"

When formulating your questions (which you should do well before you enter into the negotiation), try brainstorming with your colleagues. Many heads are better than one, especially if you're not accustomed to asking a lot of questions and are finding it difficult to think of the right questions to ask.

Don't forget the importance of tone when asking questions. It's not just *what* you ask but *how* you ask it. Asking "But why do you want that?" sounds a lot more confrontational than, "Could you help me understand why that is important to you?" Stay away from the word "but" as much as possible, as it makes your question or statement sound like an argument. Replace the poisonous "but" with a more friendly "and." This one small change will transform most statements or questions from nasty to nice.

For example, rather than say "But two days ago you said our proposal was excellent, so why can't we close the deal now?" say, "I see that you are not ready to close the deal right now. Could you help me understand what else we could do to make the decision a little easier for you?"

Prefacing your questions with an acknowledgment of what the other party has just said will show you've been listening actively and have taken on board their concerns, and using the friendly and inclusive "and" will soften the tone so that you sound cooperative rather than confrontational.

Open-Ended Questions

- Require a detailed response.
- Are useful for information gathering.
- Are useful for further probing.
- Are best used at the beginning of the negotiation.

Close-Ended Questions

- Require a limited response.

- Are typically yes or no.

- Are useful for clarification.

- Are best used at the end of the negotiation.

Five Power Questions

Power Question #1: What Are Your Goals and Objectives?

The first question you need to ask when beginning any negotiation is: "What are your goals and objectives?" The purpose of this question is to find out what the other party needs in the negotiation. In other words, what are their interests in this negotiation? When you discover what their goals and objectives are, you can ask for a list of their interests and then ask them to prioritize that list.

This is a crucial step to take in the early stages of your negotiation. It can stop the customer from pulling the rug out from under you when you're about to close the sale and they suddenly identify new interests and try and force you to make concessions. This is one of the ploys that both buyers and sales professionals use and I will discuss it in more detail in Chapters 10 and 11. Suffice it to say, if you ask them what their goals and objectives are early in the game, you'll disarm them before they can use some of the most powerful ploys and tactics.

The other reason to ask this question is that it establishes rapport. When you're genuinely interested in your client's goals and objectives, they will sense that and feel more at ease with you, knowing you understand where they're coming from and whether your two companies are on the same page. The right questions will open up the communication lines and facilitate a more cooperative negotiation for both parties.

Power Question #2: What's Your Future Direction?

The purpose of asking this question is to get more variables into the negotiation, and you can use it both in selling and in negotiating. If you say, "Hey, what are you doing in the future?" and the customer says, "We're making all these changes, we want to upgrade this and downsize that," then that means there are things they're going to need that they couldn't possibly already have. Knowing where the company is headed and what their future needs will be helps you to differentiate yourself from the competition.

A nice follow-up to the future direction question is, "Is there anything else you see for the company down the road?" The reason I ask that is to get as much as I can on the table, so they don't hit me with any surprises further down the negotiating track.

Power Question #3: Please Describe Your Decision-making Process

This question actually has three questions in one: time frames, budgets, and other parties involved.

Time Frames

The first aspect of your customer's decision-making process that you need to understand is their time frames. Learning what your client's time frames are is important because if they have time pressures and you don't, it gives you a little edge and takes away from their position.

Another reason to ask about the buyer's time frames is because when you feel there is only one variable in a negotiation (almost invariably price) and you don't have a lesser variable to concede, you can bring time into the equation.

When should it start? Will anyone be time-barred? Will it only apply at certain times? How long will it continue? When will it be reviewed? Will different categories be affected at different times? Very often issues that appear as important matters of principle today are acceptable if phased in over a long period.

All of these questions are designed to expand the scope of the negotiation. Paul and Peter's Rule of One says the more you have on the negotiating table, the more flexibility you're going to have.

In one of our recent deals, we were negotiating a three-year agreement. I started to talk about what's going to happen between years four and ten and asked if there were other things that could come down the pipeline that we could bring into the negotiation. If you have information about their time frames, you can expand your horizons and perhaps offer a fee reduction if they take the agreement from a three-year agreement to a ten-year agreement, for example.

Budgets

Secondly, it's important to gain an understanding of your customer's budgeting process. Budgets run according to accounting conventions, and you need to be able to negotiate around these. For example, in a previous chapter one party's minimum offer was $85,000 and the other party's maximum offer was $70,000. In the example there, we learned that one of the ways we could circumvent the buyer's limit was by putting the final $15,000 into the next budget cycle.

The other way to get around budget issues is to give your customers the option to pay half now and half later, or one quarter now and the rest later. Sometimes a price issue isn't a price issue but a budget issue. The customer might be saying the price is too high, but what they really mean is, they don't have the money in their budget to cover it this quarter. Price issues and budget issues have two completely different solutions.

Other Players

The third question about the decision-making process is, "Who else in addition to yourself is involved in making the final decision in this negotiation?" This is absolutely essential to your success. The last thing you want when you reach the final stage of a negotiation, after you've already put in hours of work and they're about to sign on the dotted line, is for your customer to say they need to consult a higher authority. You can't negotiate with people who aren't in the room. We've probably all made this mistake in our career. It's absolutely vital to find out who all the parties involved are in the decision-making process and get them to the negotiating table with you.

We deal with the Higher Authority tactic in Chapters 10 and 11. For now, however, just remember that as a seller you can reserve Higher Authority for yourself and avoid bringing all your decision makers to the table so that you have an out if you need it. But as a negotiator, you definitely don't want them using that tactic on you, so ask the golden question: "Who else in addition to yourself is involved in the final decision?" If they reply, "I am the sole decision maker of this company," you can say to yourself, "That's great, I'm very proud of you, but you've just dug your grave in terms of the negotiating process."

I always ask who else is involved in the decision-making process as a salesperson as well as a negotiator. Any time you're working in a sales situation there are always four buying influences involved: the purchasing influence, the technical influence (which evaluates your ideas from a technical perspective), the end user (the person who actually uses the product or service), and the economic influence (which is the true decision maker or check-signer if you will).

As a salesperson, if you can bring all four buying influences into the sales process, you will have a greater chance of winning the sale and you can put more consultative solutions on the table. It will also allow you to differentiate yourself in a competitive market if you can diversify away from the price issue.

Power Question #4: What's Important to You in a Relationship with a Company Like Ours?

Contemplate this thought for a moment: Nobody is going to be negotiating with you unless they've already made a mental decision to work with you. As a customer, why would you get to the stage where you're negotiating a contract with somebody unless you preselected them through some sort of a proposal process? So it's a good idea to ask them what they like about your proposal or your company. That kind of information can add great power to your negotiating strategy.

When you ask your client, "What's important to you in a relationship with a company like ours?" if they say "a, b, c, d, and e," you need to ask them to help you prioritize those points. I ask this question both as a salesperson and a negotiator in order to try and understand their value system and their priorities. Once you know what their priorities are, you need to keep reinforcing them throughout the negotiation and you will know which of their priorities they can afford to make concessions on and which ones they can't.

It's a good idea when asking questions along these lines to ask them why they elected to do business with your company. There might be twenty companies offering similar products or services as yours, but somehow they liked your presentation better than anybody else's, so ask them, "Why are we at this negotiating table?" The reason for this question is that sales negotiations tend to have a very strong price focus and it's wise to keep your customers focused on why they chose you. This is highlighting the value side of the equation. What is it that you really like about us? Why did we get this far? You can keep the answers to these questions up your sleeve for a future time in the negotiation when your negotiation may reach a deadlock over price.

Power Question #5: Is There Anything Else I Need to Know to Help You Successfully Conclude This Negotiation?

Finally, you can end your questioning strategy with this all-encompassing question: "Is there anything else I need to know?" The reason you need to ask this question is because you can never be sure you've already asked all the pertinent questions. You may have left something important out, so this question will fill in any gaps.

Asking the Right Questions to Test for Commitment

So you've asked all the right questions, been satisfied with the answers, then at the last minute, just when you think you're about to close the deal, the client pulls the plug. "We're not looking for new products right now," they say, or "We're happy with our current provider." What went wrong?

You didn't test for commitment! Big mistake.

As salespeople, we're born with three birth defects: The first is that .we ask too many close-ended questions when under pressure.

The second is that we always follow the path of least resistance. What does that mean? It's the path you take where you feel you will get the minimum level of rejection. One way that this manifests itself is not testing for customer commitment, because if you do and you find out they're not really committed, you might be very disappointed. It could ruin your whole day!

Salespeople would rather go with an unanswered question than get the truth because the answer they're expecting is not the one they want.

The third birth defect all salespeople are born with is that we don't listen—we're better talkers than we are listeners. I can't emphasize this enough: the key to negotiating success is *listening* to your customers. When I'm out there negotiating I'm asking questions in order to understand my client and *their* needs, positions, and interests, as opposed to telling them about mine.

Also, if you listen properly you'll be able to identify those questions that require a little more delving and those that don't. If the buyer answers one of your questions in only a few words, you need to be ready to build on the response with a follow-up question like, "Can you elaborate further on that point?" or "Could you give me an example of that?" At that point, your client might respond with greater detail and offer a lot more insight. So don't fall into the trap of nodding and smiling so you look like you're listening while in your head you're thinking, "Should I have a hamburger or pizza for lunch today?"

Testing for commitment involves asking the right questions and listening actively to the answers. Paul tells a great story to illustrate this.

His computer training company was the first one to go national in the United States. He had eighty-five offices throughout the United States and Canada, which meant he could offer consistent computer training from one end of the country to the other. He looked in the Yellow Pages for a company with a lot of offices around the country and found Merrill Lynch. He called them and asked, "How would you guys like to be one of our national account customers?" They said, "Great, that's the best idea we've ever heard, we love it. We want you to know the magnitude of this opportunity. We have 30,000 employees in North America and we estimate that each one of these people will need three days of computer training."

They were postulating a 90,000-unit order, which was just totally incredible. Then they said, "Before you draw up the paperwork, we need to have a way to market the computer training program so the 30,000 employees know it exists, plus we need a way to account for it and to administer it."

So Paul and his company ran out and created a marketing program, an administrative program, a recording program, and a tracking program. Everything was totally in place. Guess how many people went through the program in the first year? Three!

What did they do wrong? They didn't test for commitment. They didn't say, "If we do all this work, what's the minimum number of units we can expect from this order?" I don't think anyone in their right mind would commit to 90,000 units, but with a 90,000 potential they could have committed to 5,000, 10,000, or even 20,000 units.

Questioning Strategies

Buyers make three types of statements that demand a question in response: generalizations, dismissals, and distortions. You'll hear these statements all the time from prospective customers, so you need to be aware of them when formulating your questioning strategies, and have some good counterquestions prepared.

Generalizations

Have you ever gone into a negotiation brimming with enthusiasm, and presented what you believed was the hottest, most exciting proposal in business history—only to be told: "All the vendors provide that." Instantly you feel yourself deflate and it can be difficult to bounce back.

When buyers try to commoditize you, you really need to understand exactly what all these other vendors are (supposedly) providing versus what you're providing and have a nice slow process so that you make sure you're comparing apples to apples. Generally, when you're comparing your complex product or service with what another vendor is offering, there's no way you're comparing apples to apples, but the customer tries to make the services seem equal (commoditize you), because that's the only way they can make their decisions.

Any time you hear a generalization like this, have a list of questions ready about what your rivals are providing and compare them with what you are offering, literally line by line.

Following is the kind of response I would make if a buyer tried to generalize my product or service: "Notwithstanding the fact that all vendors provide those benefits, how do you evaluate how well they provide these services? How do you actually measure the level of what they provide? I'd be interested in hearing a bit more about that."

Often buyers are just resistant to change, so sometimes you just need to pull them out of that by making a statement like: "What I'm sensing at the moment is that there is a little bit of resistance in relation to changing suppliers. Is that a fair statement?"

Depending on their answer, you could follow with something like: "I wouldn't ask you to change just for the sake of change; that would be ridiculous. However, based on our discussions to date, you did say to me you were with a different supplier five years ago, is that correct? So, when you made the decision to change from your last to your current supplier that change obviously bought about benefit for your business. Correct? If that's true, wouldn't it prove productive to at least explore if the same change again would bring about the same sort of added value?"

Dismissals

"We love working with the competition." Ever heard that one? They might not know a thing about your company and they're already overlooking you. What you need to do is get them to stop thinking about why they like the competition, because you could get into a dangerous discussion with that one. You need to find out if there are any areas where you can offer something they're not getting or improve on what they are getting. The reason they are shopping around is that they need something they don't already have, so if you can work out what that is and provide it, they'll soon be telling everyone how much they love working with you instead of the competition!

Following is the kind of conversation I would have with a buyer who claimed to prefer the competition: "What are the things you like most about working with the competition? If you were the CEO of my competitor, if there was one thing that you would want to see changed, modified, added or deleted, that would positively enhance your business, what would be your directive?" Then I would find out what they would like to alter, delete, or improve in their current contract or relationship and that would be my selling point.

Distortions

What do you say to a potential client you're trying to negotiate with when they argue that your technology is not state-of-the-art, or you're not providing them with the things they're looking for? You can respond with some questions like, "How are you defining state-of-the-art technology?" "Could you elaborate please and give me a better sense of understanding what that term means to you and how it affects your business? "What are you comparing us to?" "What specific features are you looking for?" Find out why they're looking at the competition and give them other ways to get the things they're looking for.

You also need to find out if they're talking about actual state-of-the-art technology or the deliverables. For example, they might say, "You don't have the latest version of Windows." That could be true. But do they need the latest version of Windows if all they need to do is send emails?

If they think that the latest technology is by definition the best, our experience is that it's not necessarily the case, so the goal is to find out how they arrived at that position and offer them an alternative.

While it may feel like a personal attack when someone uses one of these tactics on you in a negotiation, it's not necessarily so, so don't take offense. Just see them as issues to be discussed and have your questions and answers ready. Negotiation is all about discussion, it's about finding out what the goals and objectives of the other side are. Once you figure that out it's easy to provide a solution.

As I mentioned earlier, one of the birth defects of all salespeople is that we talk too much and don't listen enough. We're always trying to impress people, telling them how good we are, how good our products and services are. Here's a great quote from former Secretary of State Dean Rusk that sums it up perfectly: "One of the best ways to persuade others is with your ears—by listening to them."

I feel that our role in negotiation should be largely asking questions, largely listening, and doing very little talking and presenting. I'd say in any negotiation, you should spend two-thirds of the time listening and one-third of the time talking—and a good portion of that one-third talking time should be spent asking intelligent power questions.

Account Review Process

Following is an account review process that I personally follow at the end of every negotiation. It enables me to identify what factors contributed to my winning or losing the sale and I highly recommend that you use the same type of review process in your own negotiations.

Sales Opportunity

1. What's the company?
2. What's the role of my primary contact?
3. What's the primary contact's title?
4. What product or service was involved?

Source of Prospect

1. Was the prospect from my outbound prospecting efforts? If so, which lead source?

2. Was the prospect from an advertising or direct marketing campaign? If so, which campaign?

3. Was the prospect from a trade show? If so, which show, when, and where?

4. Was the prospect a referral? If so, from whom? From what industry was the referral given?

5. Was the prospect an inbound inquiry? If so, thank the "sales angels" for this one.

Decision-Maker/Decision Process

1. Who was the decision-maker?

2. What was the decision-maker's title and role?

3. Describe the decision-making process.

4. Who else was involved in the decision-making process? What were their titles and roles?

5. What was the time frame for the decision?

6. What third party influencers were involved?

7. Did I have direct access to the decision-maker?

8. Was my primary contact the decision-maker?

Needs and Objectives

1. What was the prospect's specific need for the product or service involved?

2. Describe specific statements from the primary contact that define that need.

3. What objections were raised by the prospect?

4. What responses were used to overcome those objections?

Note: if you're uncertain of how well you understand your prospect's needs, review these questions to evaluate your understanding.

1. What was my prospect's business goal or objective?

2. What was my primary contact's personal goal or objective?

3. What was the prospect doing before they made this decision?

4. How many people would use the product or service involved?

5. Specifically, how would the prospect use my product or service?

6. How long has the prospect been in business? How long has the primary contact?

Playing Field and Competition

1. When did I arrive in the buying process? e.g. first, second, last . . .

2. What criteria were established by the prospect for the selection process?

3. How were these criterion determined?

4. When did I last verify these criteria were still valid?

5. What competitors were involved?

6. If the account was lost, who won?

Pricing/Budget

1. What was the prospect's budget or desired price target?

2. Was price raised as a significant issue? If so, when in the process?

3. What price concessions, if any, were offered to the prospect? When?

Referrals and Collateral

1. Which referral customer(s) did I use, if any?

2. Which collateral material(s) did I use?

3. What type of follow-up or support materials were provided?

Time Frame

1. What decision time frame did the prospect provide at the beginning of the process?

2. What was driving the time frame?

3. Did the time frame change as I moved through the sales cycle?

4. When did I last verify the decision-making time frame?

Warning Signals

1. Did the prospect hedge on when a decision would be made? If so, when in the process?

2. Did the prospect hedge on the available budget or target price point? If so, when in the process?

3. Did the primary contact reduce frequency of contact or become increasingly unavailable? If so, when in the process?

4. Did the primary contact reduce my contact with others involved in the decision-making process? If so, when in the process?

5. Did the decision-making process get changed? If so, when in the process?

6. Did the prospect de-emphasize the need for the product or service? If so, when in the process?

Take the time before negotiating to review your questioning strategy and to develop key, open-ended questions to ask during your negotiations.

CHAPTER 9

Power Communications Strategies

There is no negotiation without communication. In fact, you can measure the success of a negotiation by the standard of its communication. Most of us are not good communicators by nature. We need to work at it, especially when our business depends on our ability to communicate our needs powerfully and fully understand the needs of our clients.

Fortunately, learning to communicate in a powerful and effective manner is not rocket science. We can all learn how to choose the right words for the right situation, how to speak in a tone conducive to getting our message across, how to change our body language, and read the nonverbal signals from our clients that reveal their true thoughts and feelings, and how to listen properly.

Studies have shown that communication occurs on a number of levels: 7 percent is through the words we speak; 23 percent is through the tone of our voice; and 70 percent is through nonverbal signs such as body language. Therefore, most communication takes place outside of words in emotions, perceptions, and preconceived ideas that words often disguise rather than communicate.

Even though the actual words you speak contribute to only a small percentage of the entire communication, it's so easy to say the wrong thing! This is especially so in the sales industry, where your words are your tools of trade. We all know when someone is trying to sell us something we don't want or convince us to pay more for something we do want just by the words they use. Chances are, when a salesperson says to you, "Have I got a deal for you!" you run a mile in the opposite direction because you know it's going to be followed by a heavy sales pitch.

I work on a different selling philosophy that focuses not on my need to sell something but on the *customer's needs*. The pushy salesperson is a thing of the past. In this millennium, the new requirement for successful selling is to focus on creating value for clients and satisfying their needs. Times have changed and people's buying habits and level of sophistication has changed. Radical advancements in information technology mean that everything is now at our fingertips. If we want to know about a product we go online and have access to endless information from all over the world; our busy lifestyle prompts us to want things instantly and with a minimum of fuss.

We don't have to convince customers that they need to purchase an item these days: they already know that. What they want to know is if you can provide them with the best available product at the best price. Today, the old manipulative selling methods are losing out to a more empathetic way of selling.

Therefore, its crucial you learn to communicate powerfully—which involves using the correct words, tones, body language and listening skills—to ascertain what your customers really need, establish a rapport, and convince them that you or your company can best provide it. Then, part two of your mission is to continue to maintain this high-quality communication so as to create a long-term relationship with your customers.

Pacing

Your sales negotiations will become a lot more successful once you focus on creating trust and building rapport with your customers, rather than just trying to sell them something, for it is a well-known fact that people like to do business with people they like. To deliberately build rapport and trust, salespeople use various communication techniques, verbal and nonverbal, collectively known as "pacing."

Pacing requires the ability to communicate on a number of different levels. It requires empathy—the ability to see a situation from another person's point of view—as well. It helps us to build trust and rapport with our prospect, which in turn build the kinds of relationships that enable a true exchange of thoughts and feeling. Long-term relationships are built on common ground, and pacing is about recognizing what the common ground is and staying on it. Pacing is the art of getting in step with your prospect and staying in step with them.

Often in sales negotiations both parties may feel tension, timidity, anxiety, fear of rejection, caution, doubt, or discomfort. It is our role as successful sales professionals to communicate effectively to dispel these feelings by letting the prospect know *we are just like them.* By mirroring and reflecting the other person's feelings, we can both relax, making it easier to get into step with each other.

Successful pacing requires verbal and nonverbal action. The best way to learn pacing is to watch people in conversation in any situation. You will see people mirroring each other's tone of voice, their physical stance, and the rate at which they speak. I'll go into these aspects a little later.

Empathy

Sympathy is sharing a person's emotions; *empathy* is identifying mentally with a person's emotions. We certainly don't want to share in another person's emotions, we have enough of our own to deal with, but we do want to identify with theirs and understand where they are coming from. The key to empathy is to let the person know you understand their situation and the way they feel and that you are there to help because you are trustworthy, confident, and competent.

To establish rapport with a person you should do the following:

- Ask their opinion on a noncontroversial subject.

- Ask them about themselves, their hobbies, pastimes, interests.

- Listen to them actively.

- Look them in the eye.

- Mirror their rate, speed, and volume of talking.

- Display a positive attitude.

- Be sincere.

- Underpromise and overdeliver.

- Tell the truth.

- Be interested.

- Don't try to impress them.

- Tell them something personal about yourself.

To empathize with a person you must find the common ground between you:

- Sense their mood, expectations, wishes, and desires.

- Tell them how that situation would make you feel (establishing that you are a real person too).

- Ask sincerely what you can do to help.

Once you have found commonalities and established this rapport it is vital that you follow through or you will not lose their trust. If you deliver empty words without action you will never see that person again and that would be an opportunity lost.

Don't Talk Like a Pushy Salesperson

A good sales negotiator will try to build trust by avoiding words, phrases, or any language that will associate them with a pushy salesperson stereotype. Most people balk when you try to give them the hard sell because they can see that you are just out to make a sale and don't really care about their true needs and wishes. A pushy sales-person's communication style betrays their true motives and the customer will not trust them.

When you're coming to the end of what has been a good conversation with a potential client, you may automatically attempt to close an appointment by saying, "How about if we set up a time to discuss the next steps?" But this question shows you're really focused more on moving things forward to reach your goal—the sale—than primarily trying to meet the customer's needs and achieve a win/win.

But you do want to get a sale, so how do you move to the next step without sounding pushy or losing your customers' trust? If the initial conversation is good, you might provide some room for things to go their natural way by simply asking, in a casual, open-ended, unpressured way:

- Where do you think we should go from here?

- Would you be open to . . . ?

- Does it make sense to . . . ?

- Do you feel there may be some options worthy of further exploration at this early point?

- Is there anything I can do to make you feel more comfortable regarding how we may be able to work together?

Phrases like these are a big relief to potential clients who don't want to be pressured into buying. Low-key language diffuses any inherent pressure and gives the other person the message that your thoughts are not about your goal, for example, booking an appointment. Rather, you're simply asking how they're feeling so far and where they want to go next. Their response will tell you whether the two of you have really created trust.

Once you've established trust and you move further into negotiating the deal, there are soft phrases that will continue to build rapport and help your buyer feel that you are really working to meet their needs. Here are some other phrases they will find comforting.

Effective Negotiating Phrases

- Please correct me if I'm wrong.

- We appreciate what you've done for us.

- Let me see if I understand what you are saying.

- Let me show you where I have trouble following some of your reasoning."

- One fair solution might be . . . .

- It's been a pleasure doing business with you.

Some words and phrases when used in sales negotiations come across as blaming, confronting, argumentative, and negative. Here are some examples of words and phrases to avoid at all costs:

Dirty Words List

- You never . . .

- You always . . .

- Obviously . . .

- Logically . . .

- What you need to understand . . .

- The fact of the matter is . . .

- Please don't misunderstand me.

- Listen.

- Calm down.

- Be reasonable.

- Be realistic.

- We all know that . . .

- I think what you're trying to say is . . .

- If you really think about it . . .

- Are you with me?

- Yes, but . . .

The Three Most Powerful Words in Communication: *Us, We,* and *Our*

Why are these the three most powerful words in communication? Because using these words is the fastest way to create rapport with a client when you don't have the benefit of years to build a relationship. Building rapport with customers is an art, not a mechanical skill. Once you have mastered it, selling will be easy and fun. Learn not to be pushy. As I said, most people feel pressured and cautious about a pushy salesperson and by using these three words you can avoid giving that impression.

Rather than speaking in terms of *you* and *I*, which puts distance between you and your client, if you use the words *us, we,* and *our* you are talking as if you are already a team. Even if you think your client is way out of line on something, you can avoid blaming them or pointing the finger by using the phrase "We have a problem here," rather than "You have a problem."

If you are genuinely wronged by a buyer, and feel the need to condemn them, avoid laying blame and using the word *you.* Instead, explain how their actions have made you feel and your complaints will have a lot more impact. Think of a teenage girl who has missed her curfew after a Saturday night out on the town. Her mother could say: "You selfish brat, you have no concern for this family, you have no respect for me, and you are totally self-centered." Or, she could say,

"I feel very disappointed because we made an agreement and that agreement was not respected and as a result your father and I have spent the night feeling very worried and upset." Which response would get the best reaction? The second example would probably encourage the teenager to open up and explain her actions, perhaps even apologize. But the first one would only make her feel attacked and defensive.

Two More of the Most Powerful Words in Communication

I'm sorry. It's amazing how simple these two small words are, yet how difficult it can be to say them. It's even more amazing how they can change a negotiation in an instant, whether it's a negotiation between buyer and seller, husband and wife, or employee and employer.

If you're having trouble in a negotiation, perhaps you're deadlocked or your buyer is angry at your refusal to lower your price any further, try saying, "I'm sorry you feel that way." You're not taking or appointing any blame, you're simply acknowledging that they're not feeling great about something and you're sorry they're not feeling great. Sometimes that's all it takes to melt someone's armor and bring them back to the negotiating table.

No Waffling!

Isn't it frustrating when you're trying to negotiate with someone who goes on and on, gets sidetracked, tells too many stories, makes vague or indecisive statements, and takes forever to answer a simple question? If you're a busy person, you don't want to waste time negotiating with an insipid and weak communicator who is afraid to just spit it out and say what they want. And neither will anyone want to do business with you if you communicate in that manner.

Don't try and soften your proposals with phrases like "I just kind of . . . ," "I sort of . . . ," "Um, well I guess . . . ," and don't use indecisive phrases like "Maybe I could . . ." or "I'll see if I can try to . . ." This type of communication does not command respect and is one thing you definitely need if you're aiming to negotiate a win/win.

Conversely, have you ever felt bowled over by an aggressive communicator who fires words at you like missiles and doesn't even take a breath or wait for your answer? They love the sound of their own voice so much you feel as though you may as well not even be in the room, right?

If you want to be a powerful communicator, someone who easily conveys their purpose through carefully chosen words, you need to learn how to speak clearly and concisely.

Speed, Tone, and Volume

Of course, it's not just *what* you say but *how* you say it that conveys your meaning. If your tone is pushy or aggressive, those words you carefully chose to come across as cooperative and friendly will be obfuscated by your tone. You should aim to sound assertive without speaking so loud as to overpower your client or so soft that you seem timid. Your voice level should pace (that is, mirror) your prospect's. Aim to sound like them—don't mimic, but pace their speech level and attune yourself to it. If you talk too fast you might be seen to be nervous or in a hurry. When you talk too slowly you could be seen to be less intelligent and not sure of what is happening. You must be able to change your tempo, voice level, and tonality to match your prospect's.

The breathing rate is important in sales negotiations. You can tell what sort of emotional state you are in by paying attention to your breathing. When you are excited you breathe faster. This can give the wrong impression to your prospect, so relax and breathe at a steady rate. Listen to your prospect's breathing and breathe in pace with them. When you breathe in synchrony with the other person, the subliminal message is that you are just like them.

Body Language

You're giving what you think is a great presentation yet your prospect is twiddling their thumbs or fiddling with their pen. What does that tell you? You're negotiating price and your prospect is leaning away from you, eyes wide, jaw firm. Are they comfortable with the price? In the first case you'd probably assume they're a little distracted, which means your presentation isn't quite as slick as you thought. In the second case, they're either totally freaked out about your price or they're pretending to be.

While most of us can sense what another person's body language is telling us, we are usually too caught up in what we're saying and how our presentation is sounding to think about our own body language. But since a great deal of what we communicate to our buyers comes through our body language, it's crucial to be aware of the signals we send. It takes skill to be in control of your body language, to send the right signals—and, especially, to avoid sending the wrong ones. It also takes skill to learn to read the subtle body language of your clients.

Body language amplifies our verbal message. It can also emphasize it, contradict it, or anticipate it. Try watching a television program or movie with the volume turned down and see just how much you can understand about the storyline without hearing the script.

Body language will tell you if there is trust and confidence between you and your prospect. If you want to promote a feeling of comfort and cooperation, reflect and mirror their body language. If they tilt their head to the side, you tilt your head to the side. If they sit back and put a foot over a knee in a relaxed way, you can casually do the same.

Remember when you're trying to read body language that it can vary from culture to culture. A smile can mean joy in one country and embarrassment in another. If you're doing business with someone from another culture, read up on what certain gestures mean in that country.

Posture is also a part of body language and good posture projects strength and confidence. Sit upright and don't slouch when standing.

Reading Nonverbal Behaviors

Since you probably can't read your client's mind, you need to watch their nonverbal communication as well as listen to what they say in order to understand where they're really coming from. We have all heard that an action such as leaning back may imply hostility on the part of the buyer (or seller for that matter). On the other hand, the opposite behavior, leaning forward would show interest and attentiveness on the part of the party leaning forward.

Direct eye contact can often be thought of as a positive sign. It tends to imply positive thoughts and feelings. Unwillingness to make direct eye contact is definitely not a good sign.

Think about a time that you have had a discussion with someone and did not feel comfortable making eye contact. Was that a positive sign or a negative sign with respect to your conversation? I would suggest negative. Remember, the ability and desire to make eye contact should be viewed as a positive sign in the negotiation.

And what about the famous sculpture called "The Thinker"? If you are not familiar with the sculpture, it is of a man sitting on a large rock with his hand on his chin. What does this imply? It implies just what the sculptor intended: thoughtfulness. The same is true of nonverbal communication on the part of either side in the sales negotiation: placing one's hand on one's chin is a sign of thoughtfulness.

And what about the converse of thoughtfulness? Have you ever been speaking to someone who was fiddling with a pen or some other desktop object? Worse yet, have you ever been sitting with someone and they keep glancing over to their computer to see if there are new emails coming across their desktop?

I don't know about you, but I find that incredibly annoying. To me, fiddling with a pen or other desktop object or looking at a computer to see if new emails are coming in are not good signs in a sales negotiation. Fiddling, to me, means that the fiddler is distracted. They are not part of your discussion, their thoughts are elsewhere. And remember, what's good for the goose is also good for the gander: If you are doing the fiddling, it will send a bad message to your customer.

Nonverbal behaviors can tell you a lot about your customer and their current thoughts. However, it can also tell the customer a lot about you. It is wise to think about your nonverbal communications as you plan your negotiation and as you move from step to step during your negotiation. It is also a good idea to consider your interpretation of your customer's nonverbal communications during the sales negotiation.

Don't Invade Space

Australians particularly enjoy their personal space (the space around you and between you and another person). In the selling environment it is critical not to invade a prospect's space, yet so many people do. Australians in general enjoy about one arm's length personal space, while other cultures, particularly European and Arabic, are a lot more touchy-feely. It is not an unusual sight in Athens to see three or four men or women walking arm-in-arm without a qualm or response from passers by.

With Australians you need to think of a strategy whereby you can meet people in the business environment with warmth but without invading their space. What you need to do is identify the fact that they are there and importantly, get out of their personal space fast—*then* actually get them to invite you back in.

Fortunately, this strategy works exceptionally well in a number of businesses and particularly in retail selling. Here is a simple example of waiting to be invited in.

Approach a customer, establish eye contact and say, "Good morning and welcome to . . . I couldn't help but notice that you're looking at some of our widgets. If there are any questions you would like answered, I'd certainly welcome the opportunity to do so. I'll be standing just over here if you want me." Then turn and walk out of their space. Nine times out of ten they will come to you and you will be able to create a successful sale for yourself.

Handling Objections

People who sell typically handle objections in a defensive manner or in a way that attempts to convince potential clients that what they're saying—their objection—isn't really true. When you challenge a potential client's objections, you're actually questioning or even denying the validity of what they're saying; you are denying their reality. This immediately triggers them to be on the defensive. They begin thinking that you have an agenda, which is to sell them by persuading them. This isn't the way to achieve a win/win.

The best way to respond to objections is by diffusing pressure and creating a conversation based on trust so that you and your prospects can determine together whether you're a match.

So, when you hear an objection, you can simply say to yourself, "Ah, here's an objection. I need to diffuse any tension that may be hidden beneath the surface, and I need to be sensitive to any defensiveness that this potential client may be feeling." When you hear an objection of any kind, in most cases you can begin by responding with these four words: "'That's not a problem."

Of course, there's more to say after that, but let's first focus on this sentence and look at what you're really saying to the other person.

Opening the Conversation Again

After you respond with "That's not a problem" in a graceful, relaxed, low-key reply, your next step is to pause for a moment to let potential clients take in what you've just said. Some people may be surprised because that response isn't what they were expecting. Let them have that time. Then, when it feels natural and comfortable, open up the conversation again with an appropriate phrase that goes behind or beyond the objection.

As the examples below show, you can then ask a question that gives the other person the message, "I'm not going to try to persuade you otherwise, but I would like to know if you're open to looking at this from a new perspective." You're not trying to answer the objection.

You're simply accepting it as valid and going beyond it to suggest more conversation about the situation that may spark a connection between the two of you. Remember, your job is to go beyond the objection to determine whether the objection is truthful so that you can then decide whether it makes sense to continue your conversation.

While exactly what you say next will really depend on the specific objection, you should be saying things like, "Would you be open to . . . ?" and "Would it make sense . . . ?" The wording of these key phrases is important because you're simply asking potential clients whether they're open to considering something new that might make sense to continue your dialogue. These kinds of statements are a way of asking permission as you're responding to people so they can realize that you're there to genuinely help them. (Here you're immediately diffusing any pressure that the person might be placing on you. When you apologize and express that perhaps you were the one who caused that reaction, the other person views you as genuine, the pressure dissipates, and your two-way conversation can begin again.)

Active Listening

More sales are lost through bad listening skills than anything else. Conversations often resemble waiting to cross a busy road. You are standing on the pavement, what are you watching? Certainly not the traffic. You are watching for a gap! People do the same in conversations. They are not listening to what the other person is saying—they are simply waiting for them to shut up so they can air their point of view. It is not a dialogue; it is two monologues taking turns. This is the antithesis of power communication.

Why is it so hard to listen properly? It's simple really. We can hear about 400 words per minute but most people speak at 125 words per minute, so we fill in the gaps with our mind. To absorb the real meaning of words and not let the mind wander requires concentration and real effort. Active listening is hard work because most of the time we only hear what we want to hear or what we expect to hear. You need to actively resist your own mental distractions and listen as though your life depends on it. That takes patience and self-discipline.

It's not just our wandering minds that are a barrier to effective listening. Noisy environments where you can't actually hear what the other person is saying, personal prejudices, and relying on memory rather than taking notes all impair your ability to listen actively.

Listen for the real meaning in the conversation. That means learning to *listen between the lines*. And when you haven't got clarification of what your prospect is wanting, probe for it. Let the prospect be the center of attention. Try to find out what is really happening inside their heads. Remember to watch for nonverbal clues and watch body language. Take notes when appropriate and do not interrupt.

To show your customer you are really listening to them, and to help you stay focused on listening, try saying small phrases like "I hear you," "I understand," or "tell me more." When they've finished, repeat back to them what they've said so they feel acknowledged and heard. Say, "So what you're telling me is . . ." and paraphrase what they've said. Even if you don't agree with what they're saying, you can still acknowledge their point. By saying, "I see what you're saying" or "Now I get where you're coming from," you're not necessarily agreeing with their viewpoint, you're just letting them know that you know where they're at. This helps your client feel understood, which is something we all require on a deep level.

Acknowledging not just what your client is saying but what they are feeling is also important, especially in a tense negotiation. If your buyer is angry, there is no point getting defensive. You need to be able to diffuse their anger by listening to them fully, then saying, "I understand you're feeling upset at the moment and I probably would be too if I were in your shoes." You're not conceding anything or accepting any blame, you're just validating how they are feeling. You'll be amazed at how quickly dissipating those emotions can turn the negotiation around.

Apart from making sure your client feels understood, acknowledging what they've said by paraphrasing it avoids one of the biggest pitfalls in communication: misunderstanding. Even when two people are in the same room, standing face-to-face and speaking the same language, it's easy for one to misinterpret what the other says. Power communication is all about listening well, understanding the other party's viewpoint, and letting them know you understand, which requires the ability to paraphrase.

Listening Skillfully

- Ask the right questions, then shut up.
- Listen to the answers actively.
- Listen to how the answer is given.
- Watch the body language of the prospect.
- Take notes to help with feedback.
- Use eye contact.
- Confirm to the prospect that you understand what they are saying.
- Use empathy and see what they are saying from their point of view.

Improving Listening Skills

- Take notes.
- Make sure you keep your mind on what they are saying and don't allow it to wander.
- Watch the speaker's body language.
- Summarize their point of view back to them.
- Ask questions to make sure you've understood.
- Pause before you reply.
- Think of your answer after the question not during it.
- Avoid reacting emotionally.

Remember, you have two ears and one mouth and that is the ratio to which you must use them: Listen twice as often as you speak. If you do nothing more than this, your communication will improve and you will thus experience far more effective sales negotiations.

Negotiating Ploys and Tactics: The Buyer

Ploys, tricks, tactics, techniques, and strategies grease the wheels of business negotiation around the world. Some of these ploys and tactics are aggressive and some aren't. Some are powerful and some aren't. Some are ethical and some aren't. What you need to do is be aware of them so that when a client tries one on you, you'll be fully prepared to counter it.

Before we explore some of the classic tactics used in negotiation I'd like to explain a major difference between Americans and Australians when it comes to buying. Here in Australia our style is very straight up. We don't tend to use manipulative tactics and we can sniff out a bull**** artist a mile away, so a tactic that might work in the United States or another country might not get you very far Down Under. The same is true in other cultures as well. So if you are selling to someone of another culture, take the time to learn specifically about the negotiating and sales styles of that culture.

The reason why many tactics don't work in the Australian market is because of the way Aussies buy. We don't like to be sold to. Australians like to say no. You'll ask, "Do you want to buy this new pen?"

Immediately they'll answer, "No." After a few seconds they'll ask, "How much is it?" Then they'll decide if they want it or not. In my experience Americans do the opposite. They'll decide to buy the product first and then negotiate the price. One of the most liberating things we teach in our sales training is this reality: Australians say no so don't take it personally—they don't know enough about you to not like you!

Similarly, you shouldn't take it personally when a buyer tries to use one of the following tactics on you. After reading this chapter you'll just smile to yourself and say, "Ah, they're using that old trick are they?" And you'll have a good response ready.

In this chapter I'll explain some of the more common ploys and tactics that buyers might try on you and what you can do to counter them.

Good Cop/Bad Cop

This is the oldest trick in the book. You see this one all the time on TV police shows. They bring someone in for interrogation and one of the two cops is very polite and gentle, asking the suspect easy questions and just gathering the information they need to do their job. Then another cop, who isn't so nice and friendly, acts like they're about to pick the suspect up and throw him against the wall. The first cop says, "Wait a minute George, don't do this, we're being a little rough on the guy here" and then they escort the bad cop out. The suspect is left thinking, "Who would I rather give information to, the nice guy or the guy who's ready to punch me in the head?" The nice guy of course!

It works the same way in negotiation. One person behaves rudely and the other person is quiet, reasonable, and professional. When you're trying to sell to a particular company you might be dealing with one person who seems to be working with you in good faith and negotiating fairly. They're rational and they're answering your questions. Then another person will come in and say, "Forget about it, if these guys don't want to meet the price, we're just going to go to that other company and we'll deal with them." Then you start to think, well, this guy over here is being so reasonable, maybe it's a better idea to negotiate with him because he's not going to drive as hard a deal as that mean person will.

A variation on this is when the Good Cop tries to play on your sympathy. The Good Cop might be a young salesperson and the Bad Cop might be the sales manager. The Bad Cop will berate the Good Cop in front of you and threaten him if he doesn't close the sale. Then when he leaves the Good Cop might say something like, "C'mon, help me out here, you can see my boss is going to wring my neck if I don't close this deal." Suddenly, you're feeling sorry for the salesperson thinking, "Geez, I'd hate to have a boss like that." This one works because it draws you in emotionally and then you try and justify your decision with logic.

So, what can you do to counter this tactic? Firstly, you need to listen to them. As I mentioned earlier, we salespeople don't listen nearly enough. You should be spending about 66 percent of your time listening and 33 percent talking. When you're negotiating and you're hearing objections, sometimes one party just wants to make a point but it doesn't necessarily need to be responded to. So you can just hear the point and nod your head; that kind of takes that point out of the picture. So the first thing to do when you encounter Good Cop/Bad Cop is to listen fully and completely and don't react emotionally.

Next, you need to have some affirming, powerful negotiating phrases ready to roll. A good one is: "We're interested in finding a fair solution for everyone." "Fair" is actually my favorite word in negotiation. I use it all the time, because the other party isn't exactly going to turn around and say they don't want a fair solution are they?

Make sure you don't allow yourself to be intimidated by this ploy. Just identify it for what it is and continue on with the strategies that you had in place. Don't evaluate the Good Cop in terms of the Bad Cop and don't fall into the trap of deciding to work with the Good Cop and not the Bad Cop, because that's exactly what they want you to do. Don't even treat them as separate people, just fire off some open-ended questions to get the negotiation back under your control.

Another way to counter this ploy, depending on the length of the relationship you have with the buyer, is to call it for what it is. Say something along the lines of, "Hey, I watch *NYPD Blue* you know, don't try that one on me!" You can say it jokingly and take their tactic off the table. It also depends on how advanced you are in the negotiation whether or not you can call them on it.

I actually believe if anyone uses Good Cop/Bad Cop they've already said yes to you and all they're trying to do is maximize their position by getting a price concession. Look for the value-add. Also, if they're using this tactic on you it means they're not very sophisticated negotiators, because they've had to resort to this old trick that everyone knows about. And believe me, there are much better ones to use without having to resort to that kind of intimidation.

When you've been in this business as long as I have you don't see Good Cop/Bad Cop being used very much because people know it doesn't work on an experienced salesperson. However, I do recall an incident recently when I was doing a deal with a large Australian retailer. The Good Cop was the general manager. I'd been having my discussions with him and it was all looking good. Then the franchisee came in and said very aggressively, "No way in the world am I paying $4,000 a day." The Good Cop asked him to leave the room and said to me, "If you could just tweak it a little we would have a deal." I didn't reduce the price, but I did give all their staff members a signed copy of my latest book. It only cost me a small amount of money but it was a value-add for them.

Higher Authority

This is a great tactic and one that I personally endorse. It works like this: All the decision-makers are not present at the negotiating table, so your client can avoid making a decision right then and there. They can just say, "Sorry, we need to consult with the boss," or the Board, or the committee, or whoever has the power to make the final decision.

Sometimes a salesperson will use Higher Authority if they have to give you bad news, so that they save face and maintain a good relationship with you. So the boss gives you the bad news and the salesperson can keep looking like the good guy.

What can you do to counter this tactic? The first step is to try and start your negotiation with the senior decision-makers. If you call in high, you might get pushed down a rung or two, but you'll generally still be within the realm of decision-makers.

You can also preempt the Higher Authority ploy by your early questioning strategies. If you're caught in a situation where they're using Higher Authority on you, my feeling is that you've had a flaw in your whole sales process. One of the most crucial questions to ask early in the negotiation is, "Who in addition to yourself is involved in the final decision-making process?" The whole purpose of asking that question is that it takes away the other party's ability to use Higher Authority.

I ask this question as a salesperson and as a negotiator. That sets me up so that when they say they have to ask the committee you can say, "Well, I just asked you who else is involved in the decision-making process and you said no one else." So you should be able to take Higher Authority away firstly by shooting high in the organization during your sales process and secondly, by asking this all-important question.

If you do happen to find yourself faced with a Higher Authority situation, you need to quickly recognize that the key decision-makers are not there and say, "Hey, it doesn't make any sense to negotiate if everybody's not here, so could we get everybody involved?" Alternatively, you could make it clear that since the buyer is reserving the right to consult a Higher Authority, you too will reserve the right to reconsider any points in the negotiation. Just say, "Okay, you go and consult with your committee and I'll sleep on this and see if I come up with any changes tomorrow."

Often a buyer really does have to consult someone higher on the corporate ladder to make the final decision. It's not necessarily a ploy, they just didn't tell you and you forgot to ask. Don't panic, it's not always a bad thing. My Australian colleague Ken met with some guys from a marketing company recently. They considered themselves to be fairly corporate. They asked him for a price and appeared to be shocked by the answer. "Is that uncomfortable for you?" Ken asked. They said they'd had a trainer in not so long ago and they only paid X amount of money. So he followed up with: "Were you happy with what you got for X? Let's just look at what we can put together for you now that I understand what you want. I'll present some ideas to you and see how it fits." One of the marketing guys then told Ken he had to take it to the Board for approval. The thing is, Ken hadn't given him a price yet. Ken relaxed, as he knew by this guy taking the proposal to the Board without a price, he'd taken ownership of it and would fight to get it approved, otherwise he'd end up with egg on his face. We ended up charging them more than what they'd paid for their last trainer and the Board approved it. So, Higher Authority situations don't always have to be ugly.

If your buyer is insisting on taking your proposal to someone up the line and you're worried the deal is going to fall through, you can try appealing to the buyer's ego. Just say, "Gee, are you sure you don't have the authority, I always thought you were pretty high in this company?" You'd be surprised how many customers will fall for that bait.

This story illustrates the counter nicely. A guy was buying an expensive suit. The salesperson said there was a special deal of half price on a second suit. The guy buying the suit said, "Gee, I don't know, I'm going to have to check with my wife." To this, the salesperson said, "You're kidding me, you mean you have to ask your wife permission to buy a suit?" It worked like a charm. The guy buying the suit said, "You're right, I don't have to ask permission from my wife to do anything, I'm going to buy every suit in the store."

So, that's a great one to use if you suspect your customer really does have the authority to make the decision. I always summarize the whole issue of Higher Authority by saying, you can't negotiate with a ghost. So get the key decision-makers to the table.

Last and Final Offer

This is one of the tougher ones. The other side implies or states that this is the last and final offer and hopes you will concede. In my opinion, there is no such thing as a last and final offer. It's just a strategy to get you to lower your price.

Here's a story to illustrate how a client can use this tactic. Paul was selling computer training and received a request for a proposal from a company that had about 70,000 employees. The company said the proposal needed to be in by a certain date. Before the date he could go there, meet with the people and ask them questions, then go and develop his proposal. If it arrived one day late they wouldn't look at it. They said they would wait thirty days to sort through the material and then Paul's company would get a fax telling them whether they won or lost the proposal. They weren't allowed to call during that thirty-day period or they would be disqualified from the process.

Thirty days had passed since the proposals had been submitted, and Paul's company received no response.

They waited with bated breath, but weren't allowed to call and ask what was going on. They looked at the fax machine every day. Nothing. It took two weeks for the company to reply. Eventually a fax came through that said: "Your company has been selected as one of the three finalists." They knew there were twenty-two companies bidding. The fax said the company was happy with all three finalists and they would reward the deal to the lowest bidder. They asked Paul's company to fax in the last and final offer.

Paul's company was already at the bottom of its settlement range, so they faxed back and said, "See page 26 of our proposal; that was our last and final offer." What happened? They actually won.

What does that story tell you? You don't have to accept these things at face value. Paul believes his company was the only one that received the fax and that his company had in fact already been chosen. The reason he believes that is because they were chosen without lowering their price.

So, when someone draws a line in the sand, how do you counter it? As I said, don't accept it at face value. They'll probably do things to try and scare you but keep in mind they've already told you that you've won this bid. They already have a commitment to you in their own minds so you need to negotiate from a position of strength.

Another counter would be to ask them what it is they like about your company? Try to reestablish the value that made them pick you in the first place. No one wants to work with the true lowest bidder. If you've ever seen the movie *Armageddon*, when the guys are taking off in the rocket, one guy comments on how scary it is because the whole rocket, with its 40 million parts, was built by the lowest bidder. That raises an interesting point: Is it really the lowest price they're looking for or is it the best overall solution? Try to get them focused back on their interests.

One way to do this is to ask, "What in addition to the price is going to influence your final decision? I'm sensing that we're down to a number in a box. I would ask you to feed back what you know about us other than the money. What are your reasons for doing business with us?" The idea is to focus on what sets you apart from the competition and highlight your unique selling points.

So, how would you give the other side a way out if they were asking for your last and final offer? You could say something along the lines of, "Are we really sure we want to move in this direction or could we talk about some other alternatives because my feeling is we have a lot to gain, you have a lot to gain, we're looking for a fair solution, is there another way to do this?" When they resort to Last and Final Offer it's the equivalent of drawing a line in the sand and you need to get them to rethink it.

If someone is asking for your last and final offer and you're at your bottom line, then so be it. The bottom line is the bottom line. This takes us back to Chapter 5, where we said that the single best negotiating strategy in the world is to have a full pipeline. A full pipeline ensures you're only going to take the really good deals.

Nibbles

Have you ever been in this position? You have an agreement with a customer and then as you're walking out the door ready to cash your commission check and give yourself a high five, they say, "Wait a minute, there's one more thing I want to talk about." Then they try to get you to make small concessions at the end of the deal to get a couple more dollars out of your pocket. You just want the deal over and done with, so you say "Anything, anything, you want one more little thing, here's one more little thing." This is dangerous territory because if you let them nibble at the deal now, they'll continue to nibble at all your future deals, too.

What's the counter? First of all, don't make any concessions. If you concede as you're walking out the door, you're sending the message to them that you're a bit of a pushover and your credibility is damaged.

Next, you need to invoke Higher Authority. "I'd love to help you with that but I'll have to run it past my boss first." You can also use the classic counter, which is to nibble back. You can say, "Well, as long as you brought that up, there is something else I was looking for in the negotiation too so let's sit down and talk about it." That sends a message that every time they nibble at you, you're going to nibble back. If they reopen the negotiation it's going to put them back to square one.

Of course, you can always just say no. If the business is closed I would go back and say, "I'm sensing from that comment that based on our discussions to date you're not entirely comfortable with what's been agreed upon. I'd like to understand why that is important to you." If the deal is already closed they're just using the leverage of that circumstance against you.

One of the biggest challenges salespeople have is their inability to say no. I understand people want more but if you've given a value proposition, you have justified the money against the value proposition, and they've agreed—then the business is closed.

Crunch

Crunch is when the buyer says something along the lines of, "You simply have to do better than that if you are serious." It doesn't have to be those words exactly, but basically they are refusing to negotiate anywhere near your ballpark.

I used the Crunch tactic recently when I bought a new Mercedes

Benz. I'd been negotiating with the dealer for four months on a changeover figure and I took him to lunch. I pulled a piece of paper out of my top pocket and said, "Let's find out where we are and see if we can't put this to bed." We were still a considerable amount of money away from what I wanted to pay. So, I unfolded the piece of paper and it was a check made out to AUS$20,000. I said to the salesperson, "If you can meet my changeover price of AUS$150,000 (his price was AUS$160,000), you can take this $20,000 now as a part payment. If you don't want to take it, then you're forcing me to go to other dealers to see if they will accept my offer." So, Crunch worked well for me as a buyer in that instance.

Paul tells a great story to illustrate how he got caught years ago when a senior executive used Crunch on him. He was negotiating with a customer who was so nice and homey he nicknamed him "Dad." Dad was a big executive with a huge office. In one corner he had the desk area and the other side of his office he had a gorgeous living room. They always conducted business in the living room area. It was a great relationship.

On this one negotiation, they finally got down to the details and drafted up the contract. There was one missing detail and that was the price. Dad said, "What price are you going to charge us?" Paul said, "Dad, you haven't made a big commitment to us in terms of unit buying so we're going to charge you this price and if you buy more we'll come back and renegotiate with you."

Dad looked at them and he was very serious. He said, "This is one of the largest, most successful companies in the world, there's no doubt we're going to do tons and tons of buying. So I want a discount." Paul said okay and the compromise he came up with was to put a formula into the contract. If he bought 1 to 100 units he got one price, if he bought 100 to 250 units he got another price and so on. Basically it was a tier-pricing model.

Dad then asked, "Which price in that whole model are you going to charge us on day one?" Paul said, "On day one you haven't even done 100 units, you've only done 1, so we're going to charge you the 1-unit price. When you get to 100 we'll recalculate." Dad gave them the same line about being one of the biggest companies in the world and he wanted to start at the lowest price. So Paul added a penalty clause saying he'd charge him the low price that he wanted but if he ended up in another tier the pricing would change according to the formula. So that was the agreement.

By the end of the year, the company hadn't even come close to the buying commitments they had made. They owed Paul's company $75,000. When Paul's accounts manager went to collect the check, for the first time in the history of their relationship Dad wasn't sitting on the couch. He was sitting at his office desk. Paul and his colleagues had never done any business with him in the office segment, only on the sofa. The accounts manager walked in, a little nervous because he knew something was different.

Dad said, "Have you ever watched the golfers and the baseball players? They always do the same thing. They have a routine where they scrape their left leg three times and their right leg three times and they do this with the bat two times and they do it exactly the same way every time?" Then he said to the accounts manager, "Business executives are also like that. I attribute my success in this company to this pen." He pulled out a beautiful gold pen and said, "I sign all my major deals with this pen. He said that's what I'm going to sign your check with." He pulled out the check and it was made out to Paul's company for $75,000.

Next, Dad said to the account manager, "Here's my problem. The pen is low on ink. I can't get any more ink. There's enough ink in the pen to write two words." He then pulled out a bidder's list for a huge contract for the following year. "I could either sign my name on this check or I could put your name on the bidder's list for next year because your name isn't on it right now," he said. "There's only enough ink in the pen to do one or the other." He even gave one more caveat. He said, "You guys did a great job on the last one; quite frankly you're a shoe-in to win this other bid."

So, what do you think the accounts manager did? He ran out of the office with his cell phone, called Paul and told him the story. Paul said, "If your dad needed $75,000 and you had it in your pocket would you give it to him? Of course you would. Tell Dad, no problem, what's $75,000 among family?" After all, he was pretty much like family. So the accounts manager told Dad to rip up the check and put their name on the bidder's list for next year's proposal. What happened? Things changed at the company and they never wound up issuing that bid, so Paul's company lost the $75,000 and never even submitted a new bid.

This is a great example of the Crunch tactic and the best way to counter it is to always test for commitment. Don't give up something until you have a commitment on the part of the customer. The appropriate response in that scenario should have been, "Dad, sign the check because that's what you agreed to when we were sitting on the sofa—and put our name on the bidder's list, because you know we're the best company."

So, the moral of the story is, always test for commitment. Why don't we? Because of our birth defect: We're afraid of what the answer is going to be. It's totally crucial that you test for commitment because if you test for it and get rejected, that's bad. But if you don't test for it and get rejected, then that's usually worse. At least Paul would have known where he stood if his accounts manager had put another pen on the table and told Dad to sign the check as well as putting their name on the bidder's list.

Some people might look at Dad's behavior as unethical, but my feeling as a salesperson is that you shouldn't hold it against a person when he or she behaves unethically. Maybe it wasn't the best way to behave but it shouldn't stop you from doing business with them in the future. Just learn the lesson that you have to do business with them differently in the future.

Paul had to lick his wounds for a while after the Dad experience, but two years later he got a call from Dad about the proposal that never got issued. It was back on the drawing board and bigger than before. Dad wanted to work with Paul again, but this time Paul told him the $75,000 was outstanding and he was able to negotiate a prepaid contract. You might be thinking, was this guy crazy? Dad did a huge number on him. But when you stop calling on a company of that magnitude in the marketplace you're generally going to be hurting yourself, not them. Dad's company wasn't exactly going to go out of business. But the smart thing that Paul did do was say, next time an opportunity comes up with dear old Dad or anybody in that company, we need to negotiate differently; prepaid contracts have to be the standard way of doing business with those guys. So, the story ended happily ever after.

Remember, to avoid being a victim of a buyer using the Crunch ploy, plan out your response in advance. Also, ask more questions to ascertain the buyer's level of commitment. Then, don't be intimidated. Defend your position as firmly as possible and hold onto your concessions as long as possible. Don't give too much away for fear of losing the deal. And last but not least, if in doubt, use your own Higher Authority.

Humble and Helpless

Sometimes you'll meet someone in a negotiation that absolutely hates—or pretends to hate—negotiating. They'll try and invoke your sympathy by saying things like, "Boy, I really hate this negotiating thing, don't you?" What they're doing is using the Humble and Helpless ploy, hoping you'll say to yourself, "This poor person, they really don't enjoy this, I'd better go easy on them."

So, how do you counter this ploy? Just do it back to them. All you need to say is, "Gee, I hate it as well, why don't we work out something that's fair for both of us?" Don't be fooled. They're just playing on your sympathy, relying on your pity to get the deal across the line. This is not a bad tactic to use if it's a once-off deal, but not if you expect to have an ongoing relationship with a client as you'll never be on equal terms.

Straw Man

This is our favorite. Straw Man is where the buyer (or seller) has a list of the important points in their negotiation and they include a few decoy issues at the bottom of the list that aren't terribly important to them. No one wants to have to make concessions in a negotiation on the most important points, so to minimize that, they invent a few freebies to give away when they have to make concessions. It's not terribly painful for them, but it looks to you like they're compromising because you don't know what's important to them and what's not. They begrudgingly let you have a few of the small concessions so that when it comes to the most important issues, they tell you they already made enough concessions and can't make any more.

How do you counter Straw Man when a buyer tries it on you? Make sure you do your probing in advance. If, at the beginning of the negotiation, you ask them what their goals and objectives are, that takes away their ability to use Straw Man. Find out what their priorities are and more importantly, why. If you can find out why each of their issues is important, it will allow you to see through any false or "straw" issues.

If they said their goals are A, B and C and you said, "Could you help me prioritize those?" and they said A is 1, B is 2 and C is 3, and then all of a sudden they start posturing that C is very important, then you would simply say "Two days ago when I asked you this you said that A was very important, now you're saying C is really important. So tell me, what's really important?"

You should be able to take Straw Man away from them by asking two really good questions: 1) "What are your goals and objectives in the negotiating process, and can you help me prioritize those?" 2) "What points are you looking for in a relationship in a company like ours, and can you help me prioritize those?" That should take away some of the straw issues they put out at a later point in time.

As I said earlier, the questioning process is really important to your success because if you have good questions you can preempt a lot of the more powerful negotiating ploys they might try to use on you.

Cherry-Picking

This is a very common ploy. You will propose a deal and the buyer will "cherry-pick" it, which means they'll just take bits and pieces at the discounted rate. They might tell you your competitor is offering a simi- lar deal to yours but with value-adds that make your proposal look inferior. In reality, what they've probably done is cherry-picked your competitor's proposal in order to persuade you to give them what they want.

The best way to counter this is to ask them who offered this re- markable deal and then verify their claim by contacting your competi- tor and trying to find out if the deal is bona fide. Then, if you do need to make concessions, explain that you'll also need some concessions in return for the deal to be worthwhile to you. You can preempt this type of behavior by doing some regular market research into the kinds of deals your competitors are offering.

One industry where we find a lot of cherry-picking is IT. When IT clients start saying, "We'll have a little bit from here and a little bit from there" I say, "We priced it based on a project lot. For this project, here is the solution; this is how much it will cost." Stand your ground and say, "That particular line is cheap only because we're looking at the bottom line price for the entire package, not at individual items. If you want to look at individual items, there's not a problem in the world. Let me just recalculate the figures."

If we give someone a discount on an item we always make sure they know how much that discount is in dollars. When you prepare a proposal where a lot of components are involved, you would be insane if you didn't include on the quote the real value of each item and the fact that your price is based on project lot. Then, if the customer comes back to you and says they only want bits and pieces, you say, "Not a problem, but you can't have them at that price."

If you want a foolproof way of preventing a client from cherry- picking your proposal, make sure you specify the terms at the begin- ning of the sale. Just write the following words into every proposal you make: "The pricing in this proposal is predicated on acceptance of the entire offer." Then, if they start cherry-picking you, you just point to that one sentence and say, "You know, our pricing was contingent on you taking product A, B and C, so you either do that or we're going to have to go back and recalculate for the one thing you do want."

Your proposals should also include something along the lines of:

"The pricing in this proposal is only valid for a period of thirty days (or sixty or ninety days)." I've actually seen customers come out of the woodwork asking for prices that had been proposed two or three years before and now the pricing structure is totally different.

Those two sentences will save you lots of aggravation and headache.

Telephone Deals

What do you do if a potential buyer calls you up totally out of the blue and says, "We want to buy a hundred units, give me your best price." How do you counter that rather hurried inquiry?

First, you can avoid getting caught off guard by using a buffer, such as an assistant or voice mail. That way you'll always have time up your sleeve to prepare some questions for the buyer.

If you do happen to answer the phone and it's a local customer, it's preferable to go to their office for a meeting rather than talk on the phone. Here are a few ideas that you can use to stimulate conversations and push for a face-to-face meeting:

- "My special reason for wanting to meet with you, Jack, is to share an idea that many of our clients tell us . . . (e.g., that our particular pricing structure is the most competitive in the market place)."

- "Jack, you're really going to appreciate what our (product or service) will really do for you."

- "How important is it to you, Jack, to (increase profits, deal with a professional outfit, etc.)?"

If it's a remote client and its not practical to get in the car and drive to them, I would question them over the phone and say, "I'd be happy to give you a quote but before I do that, let me ask you a couple of questions so I can see what your needs are; then, when I quote you a price it's going to be appropriate." As with Higher Authority, you can't negotiate with a ghost, so you need to get into the discovery process, preferably face-to-face but if that's not possible, over the phone.

My company, Salesmasters International, offers corporate sales training. Many of our clients are large companies and they expect to be charged what we charge them. If a smaller company calls us and asks about price, we know they'll probably be taken aback at the full price, so we try and soften it. We say something like, "Our standard fee for our corporate clients is X." They'll say, "Just give me a price." We'll say, "No problem, we can certainly give you a price, however our corporate rate is based on material customized for larger companies. Let's investigate what you need before we get into price."

If you can keep them on the phone long enough to have a conversation, you'll build rapport and they'll listen. Then we'll say, "Let's not cause any stress about money until we see if we can do anything here. Let's work out what you need first and you can work out what the investment is." What we try to do is get them off the "how much" and into the value proposition first. It makes the negotiation a whole lot easier.

If you hear a no, an ideal response is: "I can fully understand you saying that. As a matter of fact, most of our happiest customers initially said exactly the same thing." (By doing this you automatically put the prospect with the "happiest customers" group.) "And it wasn't until I really had the opportunity of showing them the benefits of our product that they were able to take advantage of the product and go forward with it. What I would like to do is just organize a mutually convenient time for us to talk. If, at the end of five or six minutes, you don't think we've got anything further to share, I'm happy to end our discussion. If, however, you think, as many other people have, that this particular product could indeed bring you some benefits, I'd like to continue our discussions. Would you be comfortable with that? And as a matter of fact, looking at my diary, this afternoon is good for me, or indeed would tomorrow morning be more convenient for you?"

Of course, sometimes you won't get a chance to even get into a discussion on the phone. I had a woman hang up on me just yesterday. She had emailed an inquiry and I called her to follow up. I said, "I'm Peter from Salesmasters, is now a convenient time to talk?" She said, "No thanks." *Click.* We've got strategies for every type of telephone inquiry except when they hang up in your ear! Who knows what was going on in her world? Am I going to get bent out of shape because she hung up on me? No way. If someone is that blatant I wouldn't bother calling back, but if I can keep them on the line a little longer, I can show them the value of the training we offer.

If you forget all of this, just remember if a client calls and takes you by surprise, don't be rushed into giving an immediate price or a yes or no answer. If in doubt, use Higher Authority. "I'd love to be able to give you a quote right now but I'll have to discuss this with my boss and get back to you." Simple.

CHAPTER 11

Negotiating Ploys and Tactics: The Seller

Now that you understand how buyers use ploys and tactics in their negotiations, let's take a look at strategies available on your side of the fence. What ploys and tactics can you, as a sales professional, use to gain leverage in your own negotiations? You can apply many of the buyer's tactics that were discussed in the previous chapter in exactly the same way, so we won't go through them all again. However, we will revisit a few and see how they can be used to your advantage, and will introduce some new strategies specifically aimed at the seller as well.

Authority Limits

I explained how the buyer can use Higher Authority in the last chapter, now here's how you can use Higher Authority to gain your own leverage. As a salesperson, you never want to be in the position of being the ultimate decision-maker. Even if you're a one-person show, you can always say, "That sounds like a really good idea, I think I can support that. Unfortunately, I'm going to have to bounce that off my boss, it's slightly out of my authority limit." Maybe it is within your authority limit, but they don't have to know that. Or, you can say, "I have to bounce that off my board of advisors, I have a group of people I work with who guide me through my business career." It gives you a bit more time to consider your options. After you've thought about the offer, you can go back and say, "Gee, my boss supported something like that last week but she doesn't support it now. But here's what she can support." Then you can open up the negotiations a little further.

My colleague Ken took an inquiry for a national account and they were trying to break him on the money. They were looking for a concession and he said he couldn't give them one. We were about to lose the deal so he said, "I'll have our CEO Peter McKeon call you, he ultimately has the final decision." So I rang the client and negotiated an extra seminar day for free as opposed to reducing our daily investment. Another way to use Higher Authority as a salesperson is if you're not having any luck getting a meeting with a company's top person. If they won't give you the time of day, you can call and say, "Hey, my CEO is in town next week, how about we all get together and have lunch?" That's a technique that can help you get the foot in the door if you're having trouble.

If I were selling motor vehicles, for example, I would use Higher Authority to get a commitment. I'd say something like, "I'm happy to go to my upper management team and ask them to reduce their profit margins to meet your expectations, however I know that if they are to do that they will be looking for a commitment from you. The question today is, would you be comfortable giving them some sort of commitment now?"

So, this is a really good technique to use for yourself. I keep it right in my hip pocket and any time I'm not comfortable I use it.

Straw Man

I discussed how buyers use Straw Man in the previous chapter and it works the same way for sellers. You have a list of points that you are negotiating on and a few of those are not really important to you. You can give them up as concessions to please the buyer, but they don't know your concessions aren't of great value to you.

If you go into a negotiation without having this as a backup your strategy is flawed. If they want more concessions and you don't want to lower the price, you want to be prepared with something you can give up that has significant value to them but doesn't cost you much.

I was negotiating with the manager of a large call center recently and I could tell he was a bit edgy about the price. I said, "Before I present this document, I'm going to ring your call center to get a feel for what they need. That would normally cost X but I really feel I have to do it to get a feel for what will best suit your needs so I'll do it at no cost to you." In reality it cost me twenty minutes of my time and a couple of bucks on the phone and he thought it was worth a couple of hundred dollars.

But what if you're dealing with a savvy buyer who knows about Straw Man and asks you what your priorities are in order to flush out any straw issues? If you disclose your priorities then the risk is that the buyer will ignore your lesser demands. On the other hand if you do not disclose your priorities the buyer might only address your minor demands and fail to give you what you really want. By that time you have to respond to their proposal and they have the advantage.

Irritant Factor

This technique is similar to Straw Man, except that it involves introducing factors that are not only unimportant to you, they will also cause great inconvenience to the buyer. The price of you agreeing to drop the irritator is a further concession from the buyer. If you are seen to be introducing a completely new issue as the irritant, then it is likely to provoke a competitive reaction. If, however, you use an issue that you are perfectly entitled to raise, then it need not necessarily be seen as competitive behavior.

Nibbles

While you don't want the buyer nibbling at your deal when you've all but closed it, it can be useful for you to have a bit of a nibble before you sign on the dotted line. Why? Even if a proposal looks acceptable to you in every respect, if you reach across the table to shake their hand so fast you practically snap it off, the buyer may feel insulted by how quickly you agreed to their terms and will go away wondering whether they could have negotiated a better deal.

The simple way to avoid this is ask for one more small, noncontentious concession in return for your agreement. This has two benefits—firstly you improve the deal, and secondly you avoid giving the impression that you were overanxious to settle.

Telephone Deals

While you might not like your buyers pressuring you over the phone to give them a price, when the tables are turned, the phone can be your best friend. I believe the telephone is actually the most underused and misused prospecting tool in the sales industry. It can be your greatest friend or foe, depending on how you use it. You must use it daily to solicit new business. Many people ignore the telephone and its potential for sales success, yet it cuts down on travel time and costs and increases efficiency—you are able to deal with more people in a thirty-minute session than if you had to see them all personally. I guarantee that if you spoke to just ten people per day for the next twelve months *and did nothing else*, your income would go through the roof.

If you spent just thirty minutes of each day confronting cold calls, you would immediately see a dramatic improvement in your sales record. Why bother? Here's why:

The average call takes 3 minutes.

That means 10 calls per day.

That adds up to 50 calls per week.

That makes 2,500 telephone calls per year.

Let's say for example's sake that your average fee for service is just $100. Now you may hear 2,250 noes out of those 2,500 calls in a year. But you would hear 250 yesses! That means you would earn $25,000 per year by putting your energy, for just 30 minutes per working day, into telephone calls. Isn't that 30 minutes per day worth it?

Oftentimes, when conducting a cold call, your suspect will ask you to just send them the literature. This is a great opportunity for you to sort out a suspect from a prospect, and to turn your phone call around. You could answer with: "In my experience, sending literature often raises more questions than it answers. I know time is valuable . . . but in just fifteen minutes I can demonstrate how our product/service will benefit you."

The next statement is the clincher and it's very important that you say it with absolute authority, but in a soft and gentle manner: "Whenever someone asks me to send information instead of making an appointment one of two things occur. Either the person is very interested in what I have to share and wants to know as much about it as possible, or they aren't at all interested and are asking me to send information as an easy way to let me know that. Just so I don't waste any of your time, because you see I tend to be really persistent, would you mind telling me which of these possibilities do you fit into?" If they say they're not interested, you could answer with, "Thank you, I appreciate your leveling with me. And I'm sure you have a good reason for feeling that this doesn't interest you. Just before I hang up, would you mind sharing that one reason with me?" And if they say, "Send me the literature," you know you have an interested client.

Successful cold calling requires that you be empathetic, be warm, soft, listen carefully and pick up on your prospect's hesitations so you can reflect them back. You don't need to be aggressive with your cold calls—that's old and boring and you won't get the sales. Once again, be prepared to hear no. (For more on this subject, see Paul's book, *Red-Hot Cold Call Selling*).

Trial Close

The Trial Close is probably the most valuable tool you can use as a sales professional. It is a nonthreatening way to get feedback on how the prospect is thinking and what their intentions are. You are simply asking, "Is that all?" When the buyer outlines their demands you test that all the issues are on the table by a Trial Close: "Are you saying that if we were to agree to all those items, then you would be satisfied?" You are not committing yourself to agreeing, but it flushes out any hidden agenda items.

Some more Trial Closing questions are:

- What do you think of that?
- Do you like the red one or the blue one?
- Do you prefer a matte finish or a gloss?
- Is this dishwasher sufficient for your needs?
- If you were to invest in our product, would the medium or large suit your needs?

To earn someone's business, you must know what they are thinking and how they are feeling. The Trial Close question keeps you in touch with your prospect's feelings and thoughts. Use it regularly.

Either/Or

As I mentioned in Chapter 8, one of the birth defects of salespeople is that they always take the path of least resistance. This can even be to the extent that they are afraid to make a proposal for fear of rejection. One way of minimizing the risk of rejection is by using an Either/Or proposal. The other party may not like either of the options put forward but at least you can ask which of the two they prefer and so open a dialogue.

A variation on this tactic is called Russian Front. In this case you give the buyer two choices, one of which is deliberately designed to be unattractive in order to force them to choose the option which you favor. (The name comes from the wartime choice postings in the German army—any posting was better than the Russian Front.)

Goodwill: The Bottomless Pit

This tactic isn't so much a ploy as just common sense. Don't give anything away as a goodwill gesture early on in a negotiation. Concessions sacrificed on the altar of goodwill early on in a negotiation will be for nothing if the negotiation gets tough later. Goodwill arises from doing the deal, not from giving the store away. Unfortunately, generosity generates greed not gratitude.

There are indeed occasions when a well-timed gesture will generate goodwill and promote a more cooperative atmosphere, but equally there are many occasions where an unconditional concession will be seen as a sign of weakness and encourage a predatory reaction.

Weak Arguments Dilute Strong Ones

There is usually a good reason for something; for doing it, or for not doing it. Often we tell the buyer this reason. We then think of another reason and we give that as well. Then a third reason occurs to us and we add that in for good measure. The problem is that each reason is weaker than the one that went before, and gradually the original compelling argument is diluted. If you have a reason for doing something, give it and shut up!

While you should be careful not to avoid this as the seller, you can actually use it to your advantage by encouraging the buyer to say a little too much. When faced with a strong argument, ask the other party if there are any other reasons. They will not be able to resist the temptation to give two or three more, each weaker than the last. Eventually the arguments can become so feeble as to be self-defeating.

Multipoint Claim

Many negotiations can be categorized as multipoint claims—shopping list negotiations—with many loosely connected issues. The best method of handling these is as follows: If you are making the demands then try to have them dealt with and agreed to one at a time. This should maximize the concessions you win.

If you are responding to the demands then first establish their priority—which is the most important? Then link them together, trading off withdrawal of the lesser demands in exchange for conceding some or all of the major demands.

Deal Creep

When the deal has been struck and both parties have returned to base, it is normal practice for at least one of them to write to the other confirming the deal. This is when temptation beckons. You come across an ambiguity in your notes and there are two possible interpretations: One favors you, one favors the buyer. What should you do?

If you yield to temptation and put the interpretation most favorable to you on it, then this is Deal Creep. What you should do is contact the other party and summarize your interpretation to them. You will have the initiative and there is every chance they will agree with your version. If they dispute your version it is more easily resolved at that stage than in the law courts later on.

Add-On

This tactic is commonly used to increase an apparently low price: "The price of this Porsche is only $25,000 . . . plus $1,100 for the sunroof, plus $1,937 for the ABS, plus $2,000 for the alloy wheels, plus $1,500 for the air conditioning, plus $1,400 for the leather trim. Leather seats are another $1,700, not forgetting the sports shock absorbers at a mere $240."

The Add-On can be usefully employed if you realize your opening position is lower than it needed to be and you want to add a few items from your wish list.

Take-Away

This is the opposite of Add-On and you can use it to back down from an opening position that turns out to be too high. It is also widely used in the motor trade: "The price is $12,500. We are prepared to include delivery and one year's road tax. If you have a trade-in we can take $800 off that price. If you supply your own radio we can deduct another $250. If you place your order today we can supply it at the pre-increase price."

Preemptive Proposal

In some negotiations your ideal position is the status quo and you prepare by building defenses. If you feel that you are unlikely to sustain the status quo, then it may be worth considering whether a preemptive proposal might seize the initiative. As the party making the proposal, you will be able to choose the time, the place, and the issues—plus you will have an element of surprise in taking an unexpected course of action.

The First-Offer Dilemma

Who should go first when beginning a sales negotiation, the buyer or the seller? Well, there are pros and cons for going first and going second. The advantages of going first are that you set the tone of the negotiation and you'll get to see their immediate reaction to your proposal. The disadvantages are that you may offer more or less than is needed, you may lose an unintended benefit, and they may not react at all.

My personal preference is to go first. Not that there's any right or wrong, I just like to go first because I like to set the tone. Let's say the list price for our product is $100 per unit and the buyer asks for a quote. By saying $95 that means the starting point for the negotiation is $95 and you have to negotiate me down from there. The alternative is to ask the customer to make an offer, but they might start at $20 and then you have to negotiate them all the way up to $90.

There's one exception to this rule. If I sense I'm negotiating with somebody who doesn't have a lot of confidence, then I'll let them go first because I believe they might offer something quite favorable and then I can take it from there. You'll have to decide what works best for you.

Remember, if the other party makes a proposal first, don't start to negotiate with them immediately. Try to ascertain why they've made the proposal. Behind every proposal lurks a need. It is your job to attempt to understand the need. There may be other proposals which also address that need, but at less cost to you.

Where you have absolutely no idea of what you want, of the going rate, of the market price, then it may be appropriate to let the buyer open the bidding.

Usually though, you will have a clear idea of what you want. Let us call it X. Why then is there such a reluctance to ask for X? Because people think there is a 50/50 chance they might be offered more than X. Unfortunately, experience suggests these are not the odds. If you want X, but you adopt "Make me an offer," there is 40 percent chance you will be offered less than X. That only leaves a 60 percent chance of being offered X or more.

You can improve your chances of getting what you want by leading the negotiation and being specific. If you want X, ask for X. As long as X is realistic you will find your success rate will increase dramatically.

Open Door

If you are confronted with a surprise demand in a negotiation you may face the dilemma of saying yes and risk an unconditional concession or saying no and risk the negotiation becoming deadlocked.

One of the most useful techniques is to counter with "Just suppose . . ." or "What if . . . ?" This allows you to look through the door to see what lies beyond without committing yourself. Good negotiators do not close doors. They may need them later on in the negotiation. To open the door into the realm of possibilities you can say: "Let's say for the sake of argument . . . " . . ." or ask "What if there was a possibility . . ."

How to Break a Deadlock

If the Open Door fails and you end up deadlocked, the buyer's preferred outcome is often the status quo. You then have to take the initiative by making a proposal and moving away from argument. If you can block the status quo you put more pressure on them.

The first rule of thumb in terms of breaking a deadlock is to actually call it for what it is. Try saying, "We're deadlocked on this point, let's move to another point in the negotiation and see if we can make some progress there and revisit this one at a later point in time."

The next thing to do is to change from a competitive to a win/win mode. That means saying something like, "Let's try and find a solution that's fair for everyone."

If that doesn't work, then you need to look at the contract variables again and see whether there's anything you can change. Perhaps you've overlooked something or one of you can make some concessions you hadn't previously been aware of. When you're reassessing the contract, look at new options you may be able to add that could help break the deadlock.

* * *

As we've seen, there is a range of negotiation techniques you can use. It doesn't matter which technique you use—you may even use a combination of them. The important thing to remember is that if your prospect comes back with a yes, that's fantastic. If they come back with a no, that's fantastic too. Take their no as an expression of interest and deal with their objection. The important thing is to have the courage to close. It is not how much you give, but how many times you do it. If you lose the prospect, go to the next one. Robert Browning said, "A minute's success pays the failure of years." Get back up on that horse and ride to the next sales experience.

CHAPTER 12

Negotiating with Big Companies

The Allied Signal Discount

Those of you who are new to sales will probably not recognize the name Allied Signal. However, in the 1980s and 1990s, Allied Signal was one of the largest and more successful companies in the world. They have since been merged into Honeywell, but that doesn't lessen the importance of what can be learned from this story.

We had gone through a lengthy competitive bidding process for a contract to train their sales staff. Through a lot of hard work and a lot of great selling, we were able to successfully navigate the competitive bidding process and were awarded the contract.

It had been a long and arduous process and for most any sales professional, a once-in-a-lifetime opportunity. The account executive on the account was ecstatic about her good work and good fortune and thought that we were home free. After all, Allied Signal had awarded the contract to us.

This occurred at about the same time that I had started to study the science of effective sales negotiations. I had just completed a discussion of various negotiating ploys, tactics, and countermeasures. And then, I was introduced to the "Allied Signal Discount."

We had arrived at their offices for what was supposed to be a contract signing and procedural walk-through and we were caught by surprise when they started negotiating the terms and conditions that we thought had already been agreed on.

I found it quite peculiar that they would award the contract to us and then start to negotiate all over again. As I learned over time, this is a standard negotiating tactic used by large companies like Allied Signal.

So, there we were, arriving at the customer to attend a "simple" contract signing and being met by the purchasing agent who was intent on renegotiating the deal, almost from scratch. There were a number of terms and conditions that he wanted to discuss, but the most memorable of those was the Allied Signal Discount.

If you reflect on the opportunity, this was Allied Signal, one of the largest and most successful companies in the world. By comparison, we were a relatively small company even though we were one of the most successful companies in our field. Because we were in a competitive bidding situation, because we were working with Allied Signal, and because we were not the incumbent, our pricing on the opportunity was very aggressive. Needless to say, our margins were thin, razor thin! So, any talk of the Allied Signal discount was quite upsetting to me.

As you would expect, we took the time to understand what the client was asking for and one of the questions that we had to ask was "What is the Allied Signal Discount?" What we learned was that the Allied Signal Discount was a discount that we were *required* to offer Allied Signal, after all other contract negotiations had been completed (including price). The additional discount was 10 percent and it was above and beyond any discount that had already been negotiated.

As I mentioned, margins were already razor thin and there was no room for the Allied Signal Discount. Also, as we have already learned, every action on our part trains the customer to behave with us in a like manner on the next sales negotiation. If we were to agree to the Allied

Signal Discount, what would that mean for us in future negotiations with the company?

Allied would forever understand that our "final price" is not really a final price at all. Rather, it is an interim price that still has room for plenty of negotiation. Depending on how hard we made the giving of the discount appear, Allied Signal would also learn other things that could be used to their advantage in the next sales negotiation.

Fortunately, I had just done some studying on the topic of sales negotiations. If I had not done this studying, I think I would have been placed in a very difficult situation. One of the things that I had just learned was to trust in the value of your solution. In other words, maybe there was a compelling reason that the customer se-lected us.

This all sounds very intuitive sitting here reading (or writing) this book but in the heat of battle, in the middle of our sales negotiation, we are all too often willing to make unnecessary concessions just be-cause they are requested.

However, if you consider the vendor selection process, you might feel otherwise. Assume that you were working at a large and estab-lished corporation and you were in charge of making a major purchase for your company.

The first thing that you would do is likely form a team, a procure-ment or purchasing team. This team might consist of a number of people, in addition to you, that could potentially represent other areas of the company. For example, you could be in the purchasing depart-ment and your team could include the buying department head, some end users from the buying department and someone from your com-pany's technical organization to evaluate the merits of a solution from a technical perspective.

So, when a purchase decision is made, it is one that is not easily changed. In the case of Allied Signal, they went through a lengthy and detailed evaluation process. Imagine if you were on the team and you went to our meeting to "close the deal" only to come back from the meeting knowing that the chosen vendor would not be selected because they would not agree to an additional price concession, and that the evaluation process must start all over from the beginning.

I'm not sure that this would go over too well with your procurement team.

In addition, consider the evaluation process itself. I'm sure that we can all agree that any company of significance would have a detailed and structured evaluation process. The purpose of the process would, of course, be to make the best vendor selection possible. So, after selecting the best vendor, and possibly telling the other vendors that they were not selected, is it still possible to change your decision? Is it possible to change your decision from the best vendor to the second best vendor? I'm not sure that it is.

So, I had some level of confidence in our solution at this point in the sales process. After all, I realized that we had already obtained the status of "vendor of choice." This has to be meaningful in the eyes and minds of the customer. In fact, I would suggest that it is very meaningful.

Back to the story. We had just won a major contract with one of the largest and most successful companies in the world, and it is fair to say that our account executive was extremely happy about what was happening. I'm sure she was also already counting the commission dollars she would earn and had probably spent a portion of the money she would receive on this account over the life of the contract. Needless to say, she was very anxious to close the deal.

As president of the company, I too was quite excited about the deal. After all, in addition to the incremental revenue this contract would bring, this win would generate incremental business momentum for us and provide us with an excellent reference account. The best part of the win was that we had taken the account from one of our competitors.

However, as the president of the company, it was also my responsibility to make sure that the opportunity was a win/win opportunity. Clearly it was a win for the customer; however the Allied Signal Discount would make it a loss for us.

As I have already told you, our pricing on the deal was very sharp. There was a large volume involved in the opportunity and we were not the incumbent. This meant that we had to overcome a large financial barrier, the cost of switching vendors, in order to win the deal. Any further discounts would jeopardize the quality of the deal for them and make the deal a loss for us by taking away any remaining margin. The now infamous Allied Signal Discount would take the deal from one that was marginally profitable for us to one that was marginally unprofitable.

One of the other things that I had just learned in the negotiating program I was taking that I would like to pass on to you is that there is no need to make an urgent or rushed decision in the middle of a sales negotiation. It's OK to evaluate new facts and circumstances as they arise and to think through what you need to do as you come to a new decision.

So, how to respond to the Allied Signal Discount? I asked for a few moments to meet with my account executive and to think through the Allied Signal Discount.

If you were wondering how Allied Signal justified the additional discount, here's how they did it. They explained that they were one of the largest and most successful companies in the world. While they complimented our company and suggested that we were one of the most successful companies in our industry, our company was no where near the stature of Allied Signal (which was very true). When you think about it, there were only a few companies worldwide that would be able to look Allied Signal in the eye.

So, they went on to suggest that we would learn quite a bit by having the opportunity to work with them. The suggested value of this incremental knowledge was about 10 percent. Hence, the Allied Signal Discount.

While it is true that we would learn quite a bit by working with Allied Signal that would probably be true of any large company. And, they would learn from us. After all, why would they be hiring us in a consulting and education capacity if they did not respect our expertise?

We tried to explain the above but they still insisted on the discount. So, I called a time-out and asked if we could take some time to consider their offer.

The account executive was sitting at the edge of her seat wondering how I could not agree to the discount. Because we were at Allied Signal, we had nowhere to go for a brief recess so the Allied Signal personnel left the room to give us time to think and strategize about our current circumstances. During the time out, you would think that they too would strategize about their end of the negotiation given our current circumstances.

When the Allied Signal personnel left the room, I told her about the training that I had just taken. I knew that big companies like Allied would try ploys like this and there comes a point in the negotiation process where you must stand your ground and hold your price. We had reached such a point.

I went on to explain that the customer is just as likely talking about a current event on the other side of the wall as they are talking about our negotiation. If this is the case, that the customer is just talking about a current event, then the Allied Signal Discount was nothing more than a bluff on their part. If they were bluffing, they were fully prepared to accept our original offer at the previously agreed to price without any hard feelings on their part.

Can you image that!

Of course they would be quite pleased to close with an additional discount. However, what they were really doing here was testing us to see how we would respond. What the customer was doing here is not only trying to gain an additional discount, but also trying to learn about our negotiating prowess so that they could have an additional advantage in the next negotiation with us.

So, I explained to our account executive that we needed to have confidence in the terms we had agreed to, based on all of the preceding discussion.

She did not agree with me at the time but we did hold our ground. And the contract actually went off as planned. The Allied Signal Discount was nothing more than a negotiating ploy on the part of the customer!

What Can the Allied Signal Discount Teach us?

The Allied Signal Discount teaches us two things. First, it teaches us about the value of planning.

The Value of Planning

Imagine that I had not taken the training program. Imagine that I had not thought through the contingency of the Allied Signal Discount. While planning I could clearly anticipate that the client might ask for an additional discount during the sales negotiation and plan my response.

What this taught me is that while your negotiation partners (the customers) may change, the process of sales negotiations does not. The customer will likely do something like the Allied Signal Discount in many sales negotiations. So, why not be prepared.

I was.

I had thought this through and considered the alternative. I had also evaluated the potential of the need for additional discounting and knew that we had done a good job through out the sales process. I was also aware of what was recommended in the negotiating program that I had just taken. After all, to be sitting at the negotiating table like we were, the client had already selected us as their first choice for the project. The power in the sales negotiation has switched to us. We were their preferred provider and there was really no need for additional discounting. In addition, we had worked very hard to establish value in the sales process and our pricing was very aggressive to begin with.

So, I stuck to my guns. When we presented our answer back to the client, along with a list of compelling reasons why we had reached our limit in terms of discounting, Allied Signal said "fine" and they were ready to move forward with the contract. Imagine if we had given the discount. Wow!

Think of all of the unnecessary discounts we have given the customer over the years. I'm sure if you are like us, the unnecessary discounts have added up and we have left a lot of money on the table over the years.

Also think about the fact that we do not have to work any harder to maintain our prices than we do to discount. However, if we maintain our prices, we earn additional commission dollars and our company earns additional profits—all without any additional cost to the company or time investment to us.

Risk and Reward

The second lesson that I learned from Allied Signal is the notion of risk and reward. Before we actually concluded our negotiation, we began to talk more and more about the Allied Signal Discount.

What Allied Signal was telling us is that the Allied Signal Discount was designed to protect them from the fact that we may not perform up to expectation, since our company was quite a bit smaller than theirs. And *if* we didn't perform up to expectations, the Allied Signal Discount would provide their company with a cushion relating to our underperformance.

However, when you think about it, the idea that we would under perform by 10 percent is rather arbitrary. If you think hard enough, you can probably imagine circumstances under which we could under perform by more than 10 percent. Why would Allied Signal want to limit their exposure to our significant underperformance?

I asked this question during our discussion of the Allied Signal Discount and I learned that they wouldn't. Allied Signal, as shrewd business people, should really want to limit their exposure by 100 percent. And when we discussed this with them, they agreed. They really should have a mechanism in the agreement to protect them from underperformance on our part of 5 percent, 10 percent, 25 percent—or whatever the magnitude of our underperformance might be.

And here's where the negotiation really got interesting.

We also asked Allied Signal to consider the fact that we may actually overperform. If we established a metric for 100 percent measurement of success, what would happen if we exceeded the desired metric? Well it didn't take long for Allied Signal to agree that it would only be fair to apply the standard in both directions. We agreed to develop a metric to measure 100 percent of performance.

If we were to achieve 100 percent of the metric, then we would get paid 100 percent of the contract price. However, if our performance was sub par, we would only get paid based on the percent of the metric achieved. So, if we performed to 75 percent effectiveness, then we would get paid 75 percent of the contract prices.

However, the reverse was also true. There was the possibility that our performance would exceed the metric. If our performance exceeded the metric by say 5 percent, then we would get paid a bonus. We would get paid 105 percent of the contract price.

In other words, where there is a downside for the customer, their needs to be an upside for us. Never give, without getting of equal or greater value in return.

So, we worked out a measurement system with Allied Signal. It was interesting that the development of the measurement system was left to the procurement department, not the line-of-business executives who really know what our agreement was all about.

A Word About Negotiating with Large Companies

Large companies, like Allied Signal and many others, are very shrewd. They have actually set up their company structure to succeed in the sales/vendor negotiation process. What they do is to separate departments from one another in a very significant way. So, the procurement department is often far removed from the line-of-business department who negotiated the original sale.

What this does is create a natural use of the Higher Authority negotiation ploy. Higher Authority provides the negotiator with a decision-maker, the ultimate decision-maker, who is not available at the decision-making point. This allows the negotiator to defer the decision to someone who is not present at the negotiating table.

The line-of-business executive points to the procurement department as the higher authority and the purchasing department points to the line-of-business exec. In other words, they have created an internal stalemate under which a decision cannot be made because the decision-maker is never present. It is almost impossible to get the two parties together at the same time.

Next, they are set up to rely on another powerful negotiating ploy; the effective use of time. Here, you are anxious to make a decision and the customer has placed themselves purposely in a position where they cannot. So, eventually, your need to close the deal outweighs your need to gain the concession in question and you agree not to pursue the concession any further and move on to contract completion.

While we must be wary of what the customer is doing and work very hard to get all of the parties to the negotiation (on their side), we can sometimes make this compartmentalized corporate structure work for us. Allied Signal gave us the chance to do that.

The line-of-business executive had negotiated the contract details with us right up to the point of sale. We were now at the negotiating table and had agreed to our risk/reward scenario. The line-of-business executive now left the details of how we would implement this to the procurement department. However, we had much more information on how the contract was to be executed than did the procurement department. Without the line-of-business executive to help them out, they were somewhat vulnerable to our negotiating a favorable risk/reward scenario. And we used this to our advantage.

We negotiated a favorable risk/reward contract and wound up doing a great job. We got paid 150 percent of the original (pre-Allied Signal Discount) contract price.

Summary

As you can see, negotiating with large companies is not all that different than negotiating with any one else. All you need to do is follow the four step process that we have outlined again and again in this book. And, remember the principles of win/win. Yes, we must create great solutions for the customer but the sale and the negotiation must result in a win for us and for our company as well.

Conclusion

What is the essence of sales negotiation? How would you answer if someone asked you that question at work tomorrow? Think about it for a minute. You spend your working life engaged in sales negotiation, so take some time to formulate a new definition, now that you've read this book and thought about it from our perspective. If we've got you thinking along the lines of cooperation rather than manipulation, communication rather than coercion, value rather than price, synthesis rather than separation, win/win rather than winner-takes-all, then you're on the right track.

Successful sales negotiation is a sophisticated process and by "successful" we mean creating win/win outcomes. As a sales professional, it's your responsibility to develop the skills to lead your customer to the win/win, even if they've never heard of the concept. Why? Because it's easier for them to move to another supplier than it is for you to find another customer. It's an established fact that it costs about five times as much to acquire a new customer than it does to keep an existing one—so learning the delicate art of sales negotiations is crucial if you want to succeed in today's marketplace.

Long-term selling is about building a strong base for *repeat* customers (your best prize) who become the backbone of your business.

"Long-term" means working consistently over time with prospects and customers to negotiate successful agreements. For the negotiation process to work, mutual agreements must be made by both parties, and not be one party forcing an agreement on the other. "Mutual" also implies a win/win relationship.

The new requirement for successful selling in this millennium is to focus on creating value for clients and satisfying their needs rather than focusing on our need to sell something. Of course, you still need to make a profit, so your goal is to achieve a winning outcome for you as well as a winning outcome for your customer.

Of course, this can be a lot harder than it sounds. There's usually a difference between our bottom line and the maximum the customer can pay, so the name of the game then becomes *synthesizing the deal*— understanding your customer's *interests* as opposed to *positions* and pulling them together or synthesizing them to negotiate a solution. Remember, learning the difference between your customer's interests and their positions is one of the most important negotiation skills you will learn. Interests are what the customer (or you) *really* want as a result of the sales negotiation. Positions are what the customer (or you) are actually asking for—and these are often in conflict. The interests of the customer will lead you directly to their needs, and fulfillment of those needs is the cornerstone of any successful sales relationship.

Why is synthesizing the deal so important? Because no matter what you are selling, the customer will try to commoditize it and bring the whole negotiation back to price. Under those circumstances it is very difficult to achieve a win/win because there aren't enough variables to work with. The negotiation descends into a tug of war over price, and as we've seen, splitting the difference is frequently not a healthy solution.

It all comes back to Paul and Peter's Rule of One. Any time there is only one negotiating variable left in the sales negotiation, the seller must lose. You lose if you concede on price because you erode your sales margins, but you also lose if you don't concede because you damage your relationship with the customer. In order to create a win/win you must become an expert at creating and negotiating a solution that adds value both to the customer's business and to your business as well.

Synthesizing the deal is a smarter way to work than arguing over price. It's not about muscle or manipulation. It is about listening, understanding, and acknowledging. It is about working to achieve the OSNO (optimal sales negotiation outcome). If you do not understand the customer's needs or interests and instead focus only on positions, you immediately reveal yourself as a commodity seller in the eyes of the customer and you can kiss the OSNO good-bye.

In negotiation, the word "working" can have a negative connotation, like it's all too much of a struggle. Like in any other job, however, a successful process takes work on your part—and most of that work goes into planning. But if you have designed a good plan, and followed it meticulously, you'll find yourself starting to really enjoy the process because you will know how to control it, and you'll feel proud that you are working with integrity. Planning is the critical part of every sales negotiation; it's not just for beginners. As you know we are both seasoned sales professionals and we still plan on a weekly basis.

At the heart of the whole sales negotiation process is *communication* and by that we mean all aspects of communication: speaking clearly and concisely, using powerful words and phrases at the right time in the right tone, avoiding saying the wrong thing at the wrong time, asking intelligent questions, testing for commitment, monitoring body language, and listening, listening, and more listening.

Mastering the essential skill of active listening will make you a far better communicator and hence, a far better negotiator. Top sales professionals are expert questioners and listeners. They practice active listening and notice what is being said, how it is being said, and what body language is being used. They listen with all their senses. They realize they won the sale not by *telling*, but by *asking* and *listening*; by keeping the prospect involved and actively participating throughout the process.

Of course, there will always be times when communication breaks down. Often this is due to an incompatibility in communication styles.

Negotiating is all about dealing with human beings and their gamut of emotions, so you need to have a method for tailoring your communication style and your approach to match that of your customer's.

The four social styles—Driver, Analytical, Amiable, and Expressive—categorize the thousands of people you do business with into just four styles (or more if you look further into secondary styles). You can't really present your clients with a personality quiz before you begin to do business with them, but you can learn to analyze them quickly using the social styles paradigm. This can give you an advantage during tricky negotiations when you and your customer seem more like bulls locking horns than civil business people.

In these instances, when all your efforts at effective communication seem to be falling on deaf ears, those of you who are Analyticals can sit back and say, "Hey, this person is obviously a Driver and I'm slowly driving them insane with my overly analytical approach. Best I speed things up and take some action." Those of you who are Drivers or Expressives, rather than become frustrated with the people-pleasers who want to waste time clearing everything with their colleagues, can say "Ah ha! Here we have a friendly Amiable, I just need to relax, loosen up, and allow them to do their relationship nurturing if we are going to be able to work together."

Once you've learned how to apply the principles we've discussed in this book, you'll begin to experience much better quality negotiations, so much so that you may begin believing that everyone out there has the same intention as you: to create a win/win outcome. We wish that were the case, but most people you deal with will probably need to be educated on the principles of win/win.

Unfortunately, the sales world is still full of operators who are not coming from integrity or from a desire to create a mutually beneficial relationship. They're just in the game to make money—and they'll do that any way they can, even if they have to resort to manipulation by using underhanded ploys and tactics. In this book you learned what some of these tactics are about and you now have an arsenal of countermeasures at your disposal. In your planning you can prepare to defend yourself should someone try and trick you into an unfair deal.

Not everyone who uses ploys and tactics is an evil manipulator of course. In fact, you will need to learn and use many of these tactics yourself, but the difference is that you will be using them for good intentions, not bad. Using intelligent ploys to coerce your customer into an agreement that benefits both parties, especially when they are not looking for a win/win, is an important part of your job.

The Importance of Persevering

The majority of people who fail in selling do so in their first few months. Why? Because without knowledge, selling is harder than they thought, so they lose enthusiasm and they begin to lose belief in their skills and themselves.

To be a successful sales professional you need perseverance. The marathon runner and the successful sales professional both learn to take the good with the bad. They both discipline their minds and pace themselves to their own personal goals rather than to external events. They know their capabilities and know how to achieve their goals. They develop a plan for each part of the race and they train for the event through regular exercise and practice. Importantly, they recognize that occasional losses are inevitable and they see any loss as a valuable learning experience.

Successful sales professionals see each negotiation as a stepping-stone in a long-term plan. They analyze each failure, small or large, and take steps to prevent its recurrence. They see their career as a stringing together of a series of events where the wins outnumber the losses; where performance standards are consistently met or bettered—and these are the *real* measures of success.

Winning is about winning consistently over time, not about winning every time. It is almost impossible to win every time. Perseverance is about enduring for the race *series*, not just one event. Successful persevering becomes a habit that is a mix of knowledge, skill, and desire. And the desire to achieve can only come from deep within you.

Perseverance takes many forms. It includes the ability to come back fighting; accepting short-term losses for long-term gains; being in it for the long haul; being consistent, not flashy; being the tortoise, not the hare.

Caring for Your Customer

Once you have a customer, you have to do everything in your power to keep them your customer. Remember, you're dealing with people with emotional needs and wants, so customer support adds to the perceived value of your product.

It is easy for a competitor to copy features of your product, imitate a service, or utilize improved tools and equipment. It is not so easy to improve on the intangible element that makes you successful in your sales—your level of customer care. Therefore, you can use customer support as a competitive tool. Remember, your customer needs to leave feeling *served* rather than *sold*.

We believe integrity and high ethics are the basis for long-term selling success. The one-foot-in-the-door encyclopaedia salesperson would never make it in today's world. He or she would be sued for invasion of privacy, forced entry, and a host of other suits that could wrap him or her up in courts for years. "Going in for the kill" won't work either. The sales profession is one you must be truly proud to work in. Your pride in your profession will have a direct relationship to the level of personal and professional integrity you strive towards.

The true essence of sales negotiation is understanding that selling is about an exchange of value. It's not about your benefiting or profiting at the expense of others. It isn't something you *do* to someone; it's something you do *for* and *with* someone. When you put this kind of integrity into selling, you allow selling *techniques* to give way to selling *principles*. Very soon, your sales will skyrocket because people will want to do business with you not just for what you can offer them, but for who you are. Sales negotiation, like any negotiation, is really all about the people. Be positive, be proud, and be principled and there will be no limit to your success.

Index

About the Authors

Paul S. Goldner is an author, speaker, and entrepreneur. He is the author of *Red-Hot Cold Call Selling: Prospecting Techniques That Pay Off! Second Edition*. Shortly after its original release in 1995, *Red-Hot Cold Call Selling* was selected by Executive Book Summaries as one of the best business publications of the year. Mr. Goldner is also the author of *Red-Hot Customers: How to Get Them, How to Keep Them*. *Red-Hot Customers* has been endorsed by *Selling Power* magazine and every major professional selling organization. Mr. Goldner is a sought-after speaker, trainer, and consultant. His sales and motivational programs have energized audiences throughout the world. In addition to providing his programs to corporations, Mr. Goldner has appeared on CNBC's *How to Succeed in Business*, has been quoted in the *Wall Street Journal*, and has presented at the national conference of the American Society for Training and Development. Mr. Goldner is also a frequent speaker at the American Management Association, and is a member of both the National Speakers Association and Toastmasters International.

Peter McKeon is an international trainer and public speaker, and is recognized as a leader in improving sales skills. He has shared a platform with Tom Hopkins, E. James Rohn, Brian Tracy, and Dr. Denis Waitley. Mr. McKeon has worked with many of Australasia's top companies, and is recognized for his practical results-oriented approach and his ability to achieve dramatic and measurable results.